D1525404

*"Red-robed Daruma"*

# ZEN POEMS OF THE FIVE MOUNTAINS

# American Academy of Religion
# Studies in Religion
# 37

Editors

Charley Hardwick
James O. Duke

# ZEN POEMS
# OF THE FIVE MOUNTAINS

## David Pollack

The Crossroad Publishing Company
&
Scholars Press

The Crossroad Publishing Company
370 Lexington Avenue
New York, NY 10017

Scholars Press
P.O. Box 1608
Decatur, GA 30031-1608

**Library of Congress Cataloging in Publication Data**

Pollack, David.
  Zen poems of the five mountains.

  (Studies in religion / American Academy of Religion ;
no. 37)
  Bibliography: p.
  1. Chinese poetry—Japanese authors—Translations
into English. 2. Zen poetry—Japan—Translations into
English. 3. English poetry—Translations from Chinese.
4. Chinese poetry—Japanese authors—History and
criticism. 5. Zen poetry—Japan—History and criticism.
6. Poets, Japanese—Biography. 7. Priests, Zen—Japan—
Biography. I. Title. II. Series: Studies in religion
(American Academy of Religion) ; no. 37.
  PL3054.5.E5P64 1985    895.1'1'0080952        84–13910
  ISBN 0–8245–0712–6 (pbk. : alk. paper)
  ISBN 0–89130–776–1 (Scholars Press : hard : alk. paper)
  ISBN 0–89130–775–3 (Scholars Press : pbk. : alk. paper)

Printed in the United States of America

895. 1108
P771z

# CONTENTS

uop. 2

# ILLUSTRATIONS

[1] Mainichi Newspaper Corp. Committee for the Publication of Important Cultural Properties, ed., *Nihon Kōsō Iboku* (Mainichi Shinbunsha, 1970), Vol. 2.

[2] Mainichi Newspaper Corp., ed., *Zaigai Nihon no Shihō* (Mainichi Shinbunsha, 1979), Vol. 3: *Suibokuga*.

[3] Masaki Noriyuki, ed., *Masaki Bijutsukan Meihin Zuroku* (Kyoto: Dōhōsha, 1978).

[4] Matsushita Takaaki et al., *Nihon Kaiga Kan* (Tokyo: Kōdansha, 1971), Vol. 5: *Muromachi*.

# ABBREVIATIONS

| | |
|---|---|
| BZ | *Dai Nippon Bukkyō Zensho*, 1912–13, 1972 |
| FGS | *Fūgashū* (see ST) |
| GBSS | *Gozan Bungaku Shinshū*, 1967–72, 1977 |
| GBZS | *Gozan Bungaku Zenshū*, 1936 [1978] |
| GSRJ | *Gunsho Ruijū*, 1922–23 |
| KD | *Dai Nippon Kōtei Daizōkyō*, 1880–85 |
| ST | *Shikashū Taisei*, 1958 |
| TD | *Taishō Shinshū Daizōkyō*, 1924–31 |
| ZGS | *Zoku Gunsho Ruijū*, 1926 |
| ZZ | *Dai Nippon Zoku Zōkyō*, 1905–1912 |

# Preface

This book first began to take shape many years ago as I sat meditating in a subtemple of Shōkokuji Temple in Kyoto, listening to the rain drip from the eaves, pondering the pain in my legs, and entertaining doubts that Zen meditation was anything to write poetry about. I had already read some of the writings of the medieval Japanese Zen monks and knew that they had left numerous volumes of poetry. But it was not until I actually came to spend time in their temples trying, in however attenuated a fashion, to do what they had done, that I came to realize that their most profound insights were in the poetry they left behind rather than in the dry accounts of their lives compiled by their disciples and by later scholars. It is their poetry that provides the immediate evidence of a living and vital practice that other records of the time seem to me less able to do. While it has obviously been impossible to include all of their insights into the meaning of life in this one small volume, it is my hope that these poems will manage to convey to the reader something of how a Zen monk in Japan between 1200 and 1500 might have perceived his world and felt about it.

I will always be grateful to the late Ōgata Sōhaku, head of Chō-toku-in subtemple of Shōkokuji, for having allowed me to live and meditate in his temple and thereby to take a first small step into the world of the medieval Zen monks (Chōtoku-in was founded in the fifteenth century by Gakuin Ekatsu, some of whose poetry is translated here). In part because of his excellent English, Rev. Ōgata was chosen by the council of Shōkokuji many years ago to be the temple's representative to the West—the present state of Zen Buddhism in Japan has led its practitioners there to encourage its transmission to the West in the hope that its practice will flourish anew. Rev. Ōgata had in this role dedicated himself to a truly awesome task: the translation into English of one of the most important Chinese sources of Zen, the *Ching-te ch'uan-teng lu* or "Record of the Transmission of the Lamp of the Ching-te Era." In the course of his work, he occasionally availed himself of the presence of one or another of Kyoto's many resident foreigners, who in exchange for editing and typing duties was permitted to live in the temple with its lovely garden, learn from the enormous wisdom of its priest, do zazen under the tutelage of his son Kōshū (who is the present head of Chōtoku-in), and enjoy the meals prepared by Mrs. Ōgata, one of the kindest and hardest-working women I have ever met. I learned from her unending labor that the lot of a temple wife is not an easy or a simple one.

In 1979, I returned to Kyoto for a year with the help of a grant from the Japan Foundation that permitted me the time to make a thorough study of the available poetry collections of the medieval Zen monks and to translate several hundred of their poems. It is from among that year's accumulation of poems that these have been culled. I am grateful to the Japan Foundation for having allowed me the unique opportunity to study in greater depth the lives and works of the monks whose poems are translated here. I would also like to acknowledge the kind help of Professor Shimizu Shigeru of the Department of Chinese Literature at the University of Kyoto who arranged for me to enjoy the status of visiting professor during my stay in Kyoto and introduced me to several people, among others Yanagida Seizan and Iriya Yoshitaka, who furthered my understanding of material that was often very new to me.

Various parts of the present manuscript were read and commented upon by many people whose help I would like to acknowledge here. Dr. Burton Watson of Osaka spent several hours ferreting out errors and infelicities; Professor Martin Collcutt of Princeton University was especially helpful in setting me right on matters pertaining to the life of Japan's medieval Zen temples, and Professor H. Paul Varley of Columbia University in helping to ensure that my Japanese history was not all wrong. Professor James H. Sanford of the University of North Carolina made suggestions that were useful in preparation of the final manuscript, and Professor Joseph M. Kitagawa of the University of Chicago provided invaluable and unstinting help in the practical and unglamorous task of revising the manuscript for publication and organizing the material to best advantage. I scarcely need add that, in spite of all the good advice of these scholars and many others, there undoubtedly remain errors and infelicities that are of course entirely attributable to my own ignorance.

Perhaps more than to anyone else I am indebted to Professor William Green, chairman of the Department of Classical and Religious Studies at the University of Rochester, without whose personal interest and unflagging faith this book would never have found its way into print.

David Pollack
Rochester, New York 1984

# Introduction

The study of medieval Japanese Zen poetry is, to a large degree, the study of the ways in which Chinese culture and ideas were introduced to and received by the Japanese from the early twelfth century, eventually to become part of the mainstream of Japanese culture. Along with ink-painting, tea-drinking, and their allied arts, Zen and its expression in poetry were at first a part of the "Chinese" culture of the medieval Japanese Zen monks and faithful imitations of their mainland models. Eventually, however, they were to develop into entirely Japanese practices that at once reflect their original Chinese forms and contrast with them in ways that reveal an informing Japanese spirit at work in religion and aesthetics.

By the time Zen Buddhism arrived in Japan late in the twelfth century, it had already undergone some 600 years of development in China.[1] The Japanese, no strangers to Buddhism, had already been practicing other forms imported from the continent for more than six centuries. Ch'an Buddhism (the Chinese word is derived from Sanskrit *dhyāna*, "meditation," and is read in Japanese as *Zen*) traces its origin to the teachings of Shākyamuni (or Gautama, died B.C. 383) who became the historical Buddha or "enlightened one" through his own efforts at meditation. The sect is then thought to have passed through a line of Patriarchs usually numbered from

---

[1] Among surveys of Zen Buddhism in English, the reader can refer to Heinrich Dumoulin, *A History of Zen Buddhism* (New York: Pantheon Books, 1963); Kenneth Ch'en, *Buddhism in China: A Historical Survey* (Princeton: Princeton University Press, 1963); Martin Collcutt, *Five Mountains: The Rinzai Zen Monastic Institution in Medieval Japan* (Cambridge: Harvard University Press, 1981); and Akamatsu Toshihide and Philip B. Yampolsky, "Muromachi Zen and the Gozan System," in Hall and Toyoda, eds., *Japan in the Muromachi Age* (Berkeley: University of California Press, 1977).

The discussion that follows is abstracted from a number of standard histories and specialized works in Japanese, among which are Fukushima Shunnō, *Fukushima Shunnō Chosakushū* (Tokyo: Mokujisha, 1974), vols. 3 and 5; Furuta Shōkin, "Nihon Zenshūshi—Rinzaishū," in Nishitana Keiji, ed., *Kōza Zen* (Tokyo: Shibundō, 1962) and *Chūsei Zenshūshi no Kenkyū* (Tokyo: Tōkyō Daigaku Shuppankai, 1970); Ogisu Jundō, *Nihon Chūsei Zenshūshi* (Tokyo: Mokujisha, 1965) and *Zen to Nihon Bunka no Shomondai* (Kyoto: Heirakuji Shoten, 1969); Tamamura Takeji, *Gozan Bungaku* (Tokyo: Shibundō, 1955) and *Nihon Zenshūshi Ronshū* (Kyoto: Shibunkaku, 1976); Tsuji Zennosuke, *Nihon Bukkyōshi* (Tokyo: Iwanami Shoten, 1944–1970), vols. 2–5; Washio Junkei, *Kamakura Bushi to Zen* (Tokyo: Gakujutsu Fukyūkai, 1935); and Yanagida Seizan, *Chūgoku Zenshūshi*, in Nishitani, ed., *Kōza Zen*, vol. 3.

Bodhidharma (Japanese Daruma, traditional date of death 538 A.D.), a semi-legendary figure who is held to have brought its teachings from India to China. In fact, the real origins of the sect are obscure, shrouded in legends intended in part to gain legitimacy for the sect during its development in China.

Ch'an differed from other sects of Chinese Buddhism in its primary emphasis on the individual's personal recreation of Shākyamuni's own experience of enlightenment. To this end, the Ch'an monk sat in yoga-like meditation (Japanese *zazen*) for long, difficult years in order to still the mind and discipline the body. The sect stressed the direct transmission of its teachings from master to disciple in an intense personal relationship that effected a "transmission from mind to mind." This direct method of instruction is said to have originated when the Buddha, in the course of a lecture to the assembled masses, held up a flower and only his disciple Kāśyapa smiled with understanding. Ch'an thus held itself to be "a separate transmission apart from the Teachings (that is, Sūtras) which does not rely on the written word," an attitude summed up in the well-known painting by Liang K'ai (early thirteenth century) of the sixth Ch'an Patriarch tearing up Sūtras. Although at first profoundly anti-textual and iconoclastic, Ch'an came to develop its own unique rituals and canonical texts comprised largely of the recorded sayings and deeds of its Patriarchs and masters. Ch'an did in fact come to embrace particular Buddhist texts—among others, the *Laṅkāvatāra Sūtra*, said to have been handed down from Bodhidharma to his disciple Hui-k'o, and the *Māhāprajñāpāramitā Hridāya Sūtra* (Japanese *Hannya Shingyō*) a brief work of only 177 characters that encapsulates essential Ch'an precepts—but the fundamental attitude of the sect with regard to literature was to remain one of distrust.

Ch'an also insisted on the private, exclusive and ineffable nature of enlightenment, maintaining that it could be attained only by the individual's own unremitting labor and that it was, by its very nature, impossible to describe. Early T'ien-t'ai Buddhist texts had established that writing intended solely for aesthetic purposes was inherently evil, and castigated such writings as "Evils of the Mouth," calling them "wild words and ornate speech," meaning writings intended for any other purpose than exposition of the Buddhist faith. Still, even an ineffable state of enlightenment had to take some form of expression if it were to be verified, talked about, or transmitted to others. It was in response to this practical need that Ch'an gradually developed its unique style of nonsense words, shouts, blows and other baffling gestures, especially useful for bypassing the sort of logic represented by words. Also, given sanction by ancient Indian and Chinese Buddhist custom, Ch'an monks made use of a strictly religious verse form that might be translated as "hymn" (Sanskrit *gātha*, Chinese *chi*, Japanese *ge*). Kept deliberately as unliterary as possible, the "hymn" consisted of long, jargon-filled expositions of doctrine and faith in what the Chinese considered suitably clumsy and unattractive lines of four words. These hymns would appeal only to the firmest believer in rhymed doctrine.

## Ch'an and Poetry

By the first half of the eighth century, Ch'an's enigmatic and appealingly paradoxical style had attracted the interest of a sizable part of the T'ang dynasty (618–906) class of scholar-bureaucrat poets. Poets like Wang Wei (701–761) made more or less explicit use of its ideas (and often its jargon) in poetry that reveals a world-view colored by a Ch'an understanding of the nature of reality:

> Empty mountain, no one visible,
> Only echoes of voices can be heard:
> The setting sun's rays, entering the deep woods,
> Reflect back again upon the green moss.
> *Wang Wei, "Deer Fence," from* Poems of Wang River

Central to this poem is the Ch'an insistence on stripping away the manifold details that comprise the illusory world we consider "reality" to reveal the more profound reality that underlies it. The rays of the setting sun can be understood here as metaphor for the light of understanding that reveals truth rather than illusion; that illuminates, from an angle very different from that by which ordinary appearances delude, a mind "empty" of delusion. The poem can be called "Zen" especially in that it does not simply expound such doctrine, but uses instead a sequence of natural images to convey the sense of this complex metaphysics in what the Chinese have long considered a perfect aesthetic form. All "Zen" poetry shares this method of hinting allusively at fundamental Buddhist doctrinal concerns by the meditative use of natural imagery that appears to speak of something more profound than the imagery itself.

It was not with an altogether easy conscience, however, that Chinese wrote such poems. Many were, like Wang Wei, lay believers in Buddhism and keenly aware of Buddhist proscriptions against literature intended to gratify an aesthetic need. Another Buddhist layman, the poet Po Chü-i (772–846), felt it necessary to rationalize his poetry as "using 'wild words and ornate speech' in the service of the principles of Buddhism for the purpose of turning the Wheel of the Law." Although he bequeathed complete sets of his poetic works to three Buddhist temples, Po confessed to a friend his chagrin that it was in fact the more frivolous of his poems that were especially popular with the likes of sing-song girls, nuns and unmarried women.

During the T'ang dynasty it became the custom for literati like Wang and Po to travel out to the the temples and monasteries that dotted the Chinese countryside for the purpose of seeking edifying instruction in

Buddhism from monks, some of them of the Ch'an sect. Other more popular pietistic and salvationary Buddhist sects often adopted the "expedient" of expounding their teachings to the largely uneducated masses in
the form of vivid and dramatic rhymed stories. Ch'an, however, was a
more solitary and introspective practice that appealed rather to the
sophisticated sensibilities of the educated classes. The extant poetry of the
scholar-bureaucrats collected in the *Complete T'ang Poetry* includes
thousands of poems written to Ch'an monks as well as the collections of
several monks themselves, some of whom figured importantly in contemporary literary circles. Other monks such as Han-shan and Shih-te, whose
works are famous in China and Japan, are the very models of the eccentric Ch'an hermit still revered in Zen iconography.

In spite of the evidence of a few Ch'an monks' poetry collections,
the growing association of Ch'an monks and literati poets and the
absorption by the literati of Ch'an precepts into their own poetry does
not seem to reflect any general tendency toward belletristic involvement
on the part of the T'ang monks themselves. Even apart from the strong
proscriptions against such practices, Ch'an Buddhism was not a salvationary or proselytizing creed that needed to appeal to anyone. Indeed,
until the devastating persecutions of Buddhism of 845 and after left
Ch'an the single surviving Buddhist sect of any significance in China, it
desired nothing of the literati representatives of the State other than to
be left in peace to its quietistic meditational practices.

By the twelfth century, however, Ch'an, the most important sect of
Buddhism to have survived persecution, civil unrest and foreign invasion, was no longer merely attractive to the literati, but had in turn
become dependent upon them for patronage, protection and intellectual
stimulation, and was intricately bound up with their concerns. During
the Southern Sung dynasty (1127–1278) the Ch'an movement, till then
an unsystematized method of practice, was organized into a hierarchical
system of temples with close ties to the civil bureaucracy. This system
was given the general designation of *Wu-shan* (Japanese *Gozan*), "Five
Mountains" or five main temples.

An important Yüan dynasty collection of verse written by Ch'an
monks between 1260–1321, the *Chiang-hu feng-yueh chi* ("Collection of
Zen Poetry"), reveals that by the thirteenth century Ch'an monks themselves were skillfully using contemporary forms to compose highly imagistic poetry. These works are relatively free of jargon, and seem no less
poetic than those written by such important Ch'an-influenced poets of
the Northern Sung dynasty as Su Tung-p'o (1036–1101) or Huang
T'ing-chien (1045–1105). The poetry of these two men was especially
admired by later Chinese and Japanese monks and became their most
frequent model. Yet it is often difficult when reading their poetry to
distinguish the more doctrinal insights of the literati from the more

poetic ones of the monks:

> In the teachings of the creek's sounds,
> In the purity of the mountain's hues,
> A hundred thousand hymns came to me last night—
> But today how am I to talk about them?
> > *Su Tung-p'o: "Presented to the Abbott*
> > *of Eastern Forest Temple"*

> A cold windless night, but the sound of bamboos
> Still seems to sough and murmur through the pines:
> The better to listen with the mind than with the ear,
> I put away from the lamp the half-read scroll of Sūtras.
> > *Hsü-t'ang Chih-yü (1185–1269): "Listening to snow"*

The clumsy and jargon-filled "hymn" would remain a standard fixture in the collected sayings of the masters. But the number of poems in these collections that carry little or nothing in the way of any obvious religious burden increased dramatically from the twelfth century onward. It was this style of Ch'an Buddhism, with its close ties to the culture of the ruling class and very literary orientation, that Japanese monks encountered when they arrived in China in the late twelfth century following a long hiatus in such visits, seeking new inspiration from the fount of Chinese Buddhism.

## Zen Buddhism in Japan

Buddhism in its Chinese form is customarily held to have been established in Japan during the sixth century, and Japanese Buddhist monks are recorded traveling to China as early as the seventh. Before the twelfth century, however, the Japanese were concerned primarily with sects other than Ch'an: Fa-hsiang (Japanese Hossō), T'ien-t'ai (Tendai), and Chen-yen (Shingon) Buddhism, each with its own compendious literature of sūtras, discourses and commentaries, were the Buddhist sects patronized by the Japanese court nobility first in Nara and, after 745, in the new capital of Heian-kyō (modern Kyoto). Reports of the teachings of the Ch'an sect had circulated in Japan as early as the eighth century, and its precepts and practices increasingly became part of the repertoire of Japanese monks returning home from study in China. Many of these Japanese monks were interested in teaching Zen in Japan, but the older established sects, especially Tendai and Shingon with their jealous monopoly on the patronage of the nobility, were able to make it almost impossible for later arrivals to establish themselves in the capital. Even as late as the mid-thirteenth century, Dōgen Kigen (1200–1253), founder of the Sōtō school of Zen in Japan, was forced to locate his new temple Eiheiji in a remote corner of Japan near the modern city of Fukui on the Japan Sea coast, unable to maintain a temple in the capital because of the opposition of Tendai monks. Long after the ascendancy of the Zen sect in the thirteenth century, Shingon and Tendai esotericism (Mikkyō and Taimitsu) continued to influence the development of Zen thought and practice in Japan through the medium of Zen monks of aristocratic birth and others patronized by the Kyoto court nobility.

The brilliant rule of the Heian court nobility came to an end with the defeat of the Taira clan in the disastrous civil warfare of 1185. Although their actual political dominance had been waning for some time, the cultural preferences of the aristocracy were to remain the most important element informing the tastes of aspiring rulers for centuries to come. After defeating the Taira, the victorious Minamoto warriors set up their military headquarters in the valley of Kamakura near modern Tokyo, close to their own power base and far from the Kyoto court, where it was to remain for some 200 years.

The ruling class had long supported the Buddhist faith, and the Minamoto shoguns and their Hōjō successors continued to regard the religion as an indispensible spiritual and cultural adjunct to their temporal powers. They found it expedient, however, to give their patronage to a sect of Buddhism that lacked associations with the old court nobility, and were attracted to Zen for a variety of reasons. For one thing, as the most recent Buddhist arrival from China, Ch'an carried with it the cachet of the latest mainland culture. It also lacked ties with the old court nobility, who were positively antagonistic toward this new upstart sect with its suspicious ways. For still another thing, its emphasis on direct intuition, orderliness and frugality were congenial to the warrior ethos. And finally, Ch'an was relatively free of elaborate texts and rituals that required the profound learning and intercession of a potentially meddlesome priesthood—or, for that matter, much learning at all on the part of the often tentatively-lettered warriors.

While lower-class warriors were more attracted to the new salvationary sects that were emerging at this time, Zen became the Buddhist sect patronized by the upper-class samurai. As a religious body, Zen came to be inextricably tied to that class by patronage throughout the course of its development from the thirteenth through the fifteenth centuries, with the important exception of the occasional support of one or another branch of the imperial line in Kyoto. This relationship eventually resulted from about 1250 on in the formation of a state-sponsored, temple-based Zen establishment called the Gozan, culminating in 1334 with the first of several official rankings based on the Chinese scheme that graded temples in importance, beginning with the Gozan ("Five Mountains," the largest and most important Rinzai Zen temples of Kyoto and Kamakura), followed by the Jissetsu ("Ten Lesser Temples"), and finally the Shozan ("Several Minor Temples"). The numbers in these designations do not refer to any specific number of temples—as many as eleven temples were named Gozan and sixty-three Jissetsu at the same time—but rather reflect the nomenclatural scheme of the Chinese system.

By the time the Muromachi shoguns found it necessary in 1379 to establish a single temple office, the Sōroku or Registrar General of Monks, to oversee the complex activities and operations of this enormous religious entity, the intimate relationship between the government and the Zen sect was a major element in the political and cultural life of the nation. Officially-sponsored Zen monks played important roles in internal politics, foreign trade, and diplomacy with China and Korea as personal advisors to the shoguns. By the early fifteenth century, the culture fostered within the walls or under the aegis of the Zen establishment figured significantly in the history of art, poetry, drama, tea-ceremony, architecture, landscape gardening, interior decoration, ceramics, calligraphy and cuisine, to name some of the most obvious examples.

## Zen and Poetry in Japan

The poetry written by the medieval Japanese Zen monks mirrors their religious, philosophical and mundane concerns, as well as those of the temple world they inhabited. Some frequent themes of Gozan poetry, as we might expect, are meditation, progress and setbacks on the road to enlightenment, study, holidays and festivals, travel to China, health and illness, and in general the attractions and distractions of daily life in and out of the temples. Poems by the monks in the largest monasteries also reflect the social and political nature of the style of Zen in the great urban temples in which it seems that every day saw another occasion for monks to gather in groups for elegant outings and parties, often together with high-ranking members of the warrior and noble classes. This being the case, it should not be surprising that an un-Zen-like concern for the perquisites of power occasionally reveals itself in the poetry of monks theoretically detached from such mundane concerns. At the same time that Gozan monks derided and scoffed at thoughts of worldly fame and fortune in their poems, they were carefully chronicling officially-bestowed honors and ranks in their diaries.

The apparent theme of a Zen poem is often only the excuse or motive for its composition rather than its true subject. Like the Ch'an-influenced poetry of China, Gozan poetry is often not explicitly Zen in content at all, but tends rather to suggest by its handling of subject-matter an outlook on the world profoundly colored by Zen thought. Like medieval Chinese and Japanese monochrome ink-painting, Gozan poetry makes use of explicitly religious materials—poems about the Buddha, Bodhidharma and other Zen patriarchs, early Chinese masters, present monks, scriptural themes and the like—as well as of subjects that are not immediately recognizable as bearing any particular Zen burden of themselves, but which came through long association of subject and genre to take on Zen connotations. Zen thus came to be associated with certain landscape scenes in nature—reeds and geese, for example, or orchids and rocks, sunset over a village, fishermen on a bay. When one has read enough of these poems, it becomes apparent that poems ostensibly describing a landscape are in fact demonstrations of how an enlightened mind views the world.

One obvious effect of the Zen outlook on the world is to create a world of ideation in which the poet does not stand apart from or in opposition to his work and environment. For all the particular detail of his observation, observer merges with what is observed so that there is no distinction between subject and object, perceiver and perceived. This effect is especially difficult to render in a language like English which requires pronouns, agents, subjects and objects, tense, and indications of transitivity where the original poem has none of these. I have already shown something of this effect in the poems by the T'ang dynasty poet Wang Wei cited above. The major achievement of the poets of the following Sung dynasty (960–1278) was the distillation of the more vague and diffuse ideational framework and diction of the T'ang poets before them into a poetic world that is reduced in scale to small, unadorned, everyday objects and actions, described matter-of-factly in the words of everyday language. This is the sort of world that the Gozan monks tended to depict in their own poetry.

One important element of Gozan poetry was the introduction into Japan, and the elaboration within a Japanese context, of the aesthetic language of the Sung dynasty, especially of a quality that the Chinese called by a variety of names: withered, dry, cold, sour, cleansing, plain, thin, pale, bland—everything, in short, the opposite of colorful, showy, gaudy, rich, or ornamented. This aesthetic, in part a reaction to the verbal and emotional excesses of late T'ang and early Sung poetic diction, pared down to the very bone the languages of poetry and of the visual and plastic arts. It is a quality elegantly embodied in the spare and powerful fragility of Sung tea bowls, objects highly prized in Japan as symbols of coveted continental taste. Gozan monks summed up that taste in their critical writings in the word *kotan*, "antique and bland"; China was perceived as the source of this new aesthetic of minimalism, and the native Japanese reading of the first syllable of the word as *kara* makes a significant pun on the words "China" and "withered."

In keeping with the understatement characteristic of this aesthetic taste, as well as with a natural aversion to embellishment, the vocabulary of Gozan poetry is often laconic in the extreme. Gozan poems are populated by undifferentiated and attributeless everyday objects: desks, meditation platforms, cushions, lamps, eaves, tea-bowls, steps, gates and the like appear with such portentous regularity that they seem to assume a significance beyond that of any particular object. In short, they become recognizable emblems of an informing Zen outlook. Because Zen emphatically denies the duality implied in the act of discriminating among things, in the economy of Zen thought no object or attribute can be inherently better or worse than any other. Therefore, it follows that all objects and attributes manifest Zen principles in equal measure and are equally emblematic of them. The constant presence in the poetry of the Gozan monks of these concrete, everyday objects modified, if at all, only by extraordinarily conventional attributes—"blue" skies, "green" trees, "clear" streams—prevents their poetry from disintegrating into either expositions of doctrinal jargon or vague expressions of egoless ecstasy, and contributes to a sense that a cold, hard, bright reality lurks mysteriously just beneath the surface of the words.

While any object might thus be emblematic of Zen principles, certain objects and activities were so charged with symbolic meaning through regular association with Zen ideas that they came in time to constitute a sort of code language. Because of the almost automatic association of words with certain Zen referents, Zen poetry can often be interpreted on two independent levels of meaning in a way that is "metaphysical" in much the same sense that the word is applied to the poetry of seventeenth-century England. A poem ostensibly about a sleeping monk dreaming beside a hearth in which he is burning crimson maples leaves against the cold, for example, can also be read with the following schema in mind:

| | |
|---|---|
| sleep: | meditation—not because meditating monks slept, but because the ordinary state of unenlightened wakefulness is in fact like being asleep. |
| dream: | enlightenment, the new state of "reality" that results from "sleep." |
| maple leaves: | the illusory world of discriminations based on sensory perceptions of such things as the brilliant "colors" of maple leaves in autumn. |
| fire: | the passions that are fed by the fuel of deluded perception ("leaves"). |
| ashes: | the death of the ego, achieved by the extinction of the passions fueled by illusion. |
| hearth: | Zen, the arena in and means by which the fuel of illusion is reduced to ashes by the fire of the passions that it creates and sustains. |

The number of such words and their Zen referents could be greatly extended, but this short list will suffice to alert the reader that Gozan Zen poems are rarely limited to their apparent surface meanings alone.

Besides bearing the burden of this sort of association of words with

Zen concepts, Gozan poems often refer specifically in language or allusion to Zen parables, lines and phrases from the sayings and deeds of the masters, or even to parts of the Buddhist Sūtras revered by the Zen monks. Because there is in fact no end to the number of footnotes that might be appended to these poems, I have made an effort to annotate only the most necessary references to names, places and events. Gozan poets wrote for an audience of their fellow monks and expected their readers to understand these poems readily. It was hardly their intention to make anyone plod through reams of annotations simply to comprehend a poem that was, after all, supposed to be the expression of a profound and ineffable insight.

Most early Zen masters believed that while no amount of talent for poetry would help make one a better Zen monk, advancement in Zen practice would reveal itself immediately in one's poetry. Thus developed the tradition of writing a poem to demonstrate one's enlightenment. This idea was turned on its head in fifteenth century Japan when proficiency in poetry almost entirely usurped the primacy of Zen training in the popular belief that "poetry *is* Zen," a view that had been advocated by some Chinese literary theorists as early as the thirteenth century. The frequent warnings of early Chinese and Japanese Zen masters to their all-too-literary Japanese charges to desist from poetizing and stick to their meditation mats were really attempts to discourage the understandable enthusiasm among young monks to give some sort of expression to still immature states of enlightenment. The Chinese monk Ch'ing-yüan Wei-hsin is reported to have said something like "Before I practiced Zen, mountains were mountains; when I first practiced Zen, mountains were no longer mountains; now that I understand Zen, mountains are again mountains." It is the second stage of this process that was responsible for sophomoric Zen and bad poetry. The great Gozan monk Musō Soseki made a famous classification of his disciples into three grades depending on whether they simply did *zazen* (top grade) or occupied themselves with Sūtras and other religious writings to the exclusion of all else (bottom grade). But those who did nothing but copy from model handbooks of poetry he dismissed contemptuously as merely "frocked bums" and "robed ricebags." It was expected that a monk who had reached the third stage described by Ch'ing-yüan was justified in writing expressions of his state of enlightenment, and that the poetry that resulted from it would have a hard temper that made it ring true. As the composition of poetry in the course of the fifteenth century gradually usurped the areas of Zen practice formerly occupied by meditation and direct guidance, however, Gozan poetry often came to resemble ordinary Chinese poetry—better or worse as the monks' talents permitted, more or less "Zen" depending on the actual state of their enlightenment. The world of the major urban Zen temples of medieval Japan was a complex and busy one, full of social occasions that demanded the composition of poems. The more the monks' time was occupied with such occasions, the less time they had for Zen practice. What with arrivals and departures, congratulations and consolations, good and inclement weather and its attendant seasonal outings or lack of them, literary gatherings, tea parties, flower-viewing parties, queries, replies and solicitations, it is little wonder if monks had almost no time left for the solitary and aggravating business of seeking enlightenment.

### The Poetry of the Zen Monks

The logic of Gozan poetry usually follows the dictates of the forms and conventions of the Chinese genres on which it was modeled.[2] A glance through this volume will reveal that most of the poems are of either the eight-line "regulated verse" (*lü-shih*) or the four-line "cut-off lines" (*chüeh-chü*) types, each with its own characteristic logic of exposition. The four lines of the *chüeh-chü*, for example, respectively make a statement, develop it, turn the idea in a new direction, and finally cap it, often in a surprising way:

> Eyes filled with yellow dust, I arrived ill and weary,
> A leaf fallen from a green tree that couldn't stand the autumn;
> But having had a hot soak, everything is find again—
> If it just weren't for these horse-flies lighting on my head. . . .
> *Tesshū Tokusai, "Hot-spring"*

The *lü-shih* poem extends and attenuates this same pattern of development in units of couplets rather than lines: the first couplet makes a statement that the highly antithetical second and third couplets illustrate in concrete but often oblique fashion; the final couplet then caps the poem, again in a way that is often unexpected:

> Miserably cold, the temple before the dawn,
> Still and lonely, few monks to be seen.
> The temple is old with soot-blackened walls,
> The pond overgrown, its surface like the folds in a robe.
> Incense before the Buddha has burned, gone out, turned cold,
> The sermon over, blossoms fly in the rain:
> I've reached the point of doing away with happiness and sadness—
> A white board door swinging to and fro in the breeze.
> *Gidō Shūshin, "Recalling Old Times"*

Both *chüeh-chü* and *lü-shih* possess in addition formidable rules governing the use of tones, each Chinese character classified as either "flat" or "oblique" and used only where permitted within a few rigid patterns.

---

[2] See James J. Y. Liu, *The Art of Chinese Poetry* (Chicago: University of Chicago Press, 1965).

These rules, which evolved in Chinese poetry from the sixth century, were probably not too much more onerous to the Japanese of the thirteenth century than they were to their contemporary Chinese counterparts, since spoken Chinese had by that time changed so much that the tonal distinctions and rhyme categories of centuries ago were no more obvious to most Chinese than they were to the Japanese. Poets in both countries worked instead from rules either committed to memory or else near to hand in convenient rule-books.

Chinese poets seem to have chafed at the restraints imposed on them by these two smaller forms of poetry, and gave themselves over with relief to the larger "extended-ruled" (pa'i-lü), "old-style" (ku-shih) or "folk-song style" (yüeh-fu) forms, which seem more congenial to the Chinese impulse to give free rein, often at great length, to intense emotional states. In long poems in which, in the latter two forms, tonal rules could be ignored and rhymes changed as often as desired, Chinese poets enjoyed piling up couplets in little apparent sequence, as if once freed from petty technical restraints they needed no longer concern themselves with considerations of logical development and exposition.

Gozan poets also wrote a bit of this longer-winded poetry, some of it quite good. For the most part, however, the Japanese tended to shy away from these longer forms, preferring the much tighter logic and the restrictions imposed by the short poems which were no doubt more congenial to the native mode of argumentation of the short thirty-one-syllable *waka* poem. The logic of the *waka* builds by the technique of incremental subordination of linear units called hypotaxis, rather than by placing antithetical units side by side in the parataxis characteristic of Chinese poetry.[3] On occasion, the meaning of Gozan poems seems to spill over the ends of the lines in a way characteristic of Japanese verse but not at all typical of end-stopped Chinese poetry. One can compare the differences between Chinese and Japanese poems written on the same theme in the works included in this volume of Musō Soseki, one of the rare monks who wrote (and was willing to be seen writing) poetry in Japanese as well as in Chinese.

For all their outward Chinese appearance, however, Gozan poems often explore very Japanese subjects in very un-Chinese ways. When they read Gozan poetry, the Chinese frequently accused it of "smelling Japanese," but this only tells us to what degree it reveals the essentially Japanese personality behind the assumed Chinese mask. Even if he was writing in Chinese characters, the poet was after all a Japanese, and usually more familiar with the seasons, climate, geology, geography and flora and fauna of his native country than of China—especially if he had

---

[3] See Robert H. Brower and Earl Miner, *Japanese Court Poetry* (Stanford: Stanford University Press, 1961), pp. 140ff.

never traveled to the continent, which, from about 1350 on, was increasingly the case. Nor was it only Japanese monks who wrote poetry that gives a distinct sense of cultural dislocation. Although the Chinese monk Ming-chi Ch'u-chun lived in Japan only six years until his death there in 1336, he seems in his poem "Start of Summer" (p. 118) to reveal a very Japanese preoccupation with the failure of the Japanese seasons to accord properly with the Chinese poetic characteristics conventionally applied to them.

The Gozan monks thought of themselves as living in a "Chinese" world, and the architecture of their temples, the food they ate, the furniture they used, the language they wrote and often could speak, and the arts they produced and enjoyed were all certainly modeled on the Chinese. But, inevitably, they also wrote poems on themes ignored by the Chinese. Poems about trips to hot-spring resorts for cures, for example, figure prominently in Gozan poetry (see the poem by Tesshū Tokusai cited above) because the Japanese islands, stretched over a framework of active volcanoes, abound in such places, and China does not. The hot-springs that figure most prominently in Gozan poetry are those closest to the two centers of power, Atami near Kamukura (the seat of the warrior military government), and Arima near the ancient capital court city of Kyoto.

Conversely, some images common to Chinese poetry scarcely appear at all in Gozan monks' poems, unless a monk were writing during a stay in China. Conspicuously absent, for instance, are city walls and multi-storied buildings made of stone or brick and mortar, the wail of barbarous Tartar flutes, or the screech of southern monkeys. These are replaced instead by thatch-roof farmhouses seen over a low hedgerow fence, the aristocratic tones of the Japanese koto, or the twittering of a bush-warbler.

Nor is the landscape in which Japanese temples and villages are set in Gozan poems like its Chinese counterpart. Both countries share broad expanses of sky and water; but the abrupt scarp, the deep rivers cutting through twisting gorges, and the dusty plains so characteristic of China are entirely lacking in Japan. Nature in Gozan poetry is, on the whole, the gentle, numinous presence of the shores and bays familiar to the native Japanese *waka*, and the names of places are most often those of classical *utamakura* or places with famous associations in ancient Japanese poetry.

### Zen Poetry and Painting

Gozan poetry also has unique themes that are not explored in Chinese poetry. One of the most significant, as we have already seen, is the almost metaphysical exploration of the implications of "color." This theme is based upon the famous central teaching of the *Heart Sutra* (in Japanese, *Hannya Shingyō*) that "Phenomenal Reality is itself Emptiness, Emptiness is itself Phenomenal Reality." The phrase is written with characters that can also be read "Color is itself sky, sky is itself color" (*shiki soku ze kū, kū soku ze shiki*), and from this crucial pun follows the creation of color—and so the manifold but illusory discriminations of the senses we interpret as "reality"—at sunrise, and its extinction at sunset. Moonlight, to the contrary, is a common Buddhist symbol of enlightenment, for it has the opposite effect of reducing all color to monochrome; we have already seen how Zen poetry uses the image of the reduction by fire of the bright reds and golds of autumn foliage to grey ash. In their exploration of this theme the Gozan poets consciously suppressed the opaque, vivid colors of the palette of traditional Heian and Kamakura period scroll painting (*emakimono*) to the muted, transparent modulations of ink that characterize medieval Zen ink-painting (*suibokuga*).

Heian Japanese art represents reality in brilliantly colored scenes of rhythmical decorative quality on plane surfaces. The Chinese genre, by contrast, employs a schematic shorthand of brushstrokes to suggest the scene's underlying reality, comprised of elements that do not depend on anything as mutable as color, but rather on the very structure of the forms generated by the medium of ink. This Chinese technique was adopted by the Japanese in accordance with a native code of transformation in which "Chinese brushwork was transformed into patterns of ink which provided the scaffolding for a system of polychrome design."[4]

This summary of the principles at work in the Japanese adoption and adaptation of Chinese painting techniques during the Muromachi period accords well with the suggestion by one scholar that, in contrast to earlier concerns with the lyrical expression of emotion in *waka* poetry and with the effect of stylized pattern in narrative, Gozan poetry signifies a "striving toward self-expression through creative activity based on a life devoted to the search for fundamental truths of existence"—that is, a probing, introspective and isolating cast inspired by Chinese conventions in Buddhism and poetry, as opposed to a more native Japanese concern with pattern and effect.[5]

The relationship between ink painting and poetry within the Gozan is a complex one. Paintings were often intended as illustrations of poetic ideas, and poems composed to serve as inscriptions on paintings. Poems written as inscriptions on paintings became a favorite Gozan genre from about the last quarter of the fourteenth century, and it is partly in the relationship between these two genres that we see how the Japanese

---

[4] See Gail Capitol Weigl, "The reception of Chinese painting models in Muromachi Japan," *Monumenta Nipponica* 35 (Autumn, 1980), p. 260.
[5] Yasuraoka Kōsaku, *Chūseiteki Bungaku no Tankyū* (Tokyo: Yūseidō, 1970), pp. 53ff.

reinterpreted the semantic and semiotic boundaries of Chinese art and poetry. Poems written as inscriptions were never intended to stand alone, although for the most part they do so very nicely, and are sometimes startling in their ability to evoke the absent scene they were intended to complement. The poems were in fact considered necessary complements to the paintings, bringing an added dimension to the visual ones by exploring their subject-matter in time, historical context, motion, religion and literature in ways that could not be achieved visually or iconographically. We have already seen that certain poetic allusions were regularly associated with certain subjects, and these allusions were known to Gozan poets and artists through their common education.

Poems inscribed on paintings acknowledge these implicit or explicit literary conventions while at the same time they play against conventional expectations. Thus, a painting of a line of crows in the sky or roosting in trees would suggest the idea of "sunset" to the viewer, since from early Chinese mythology the sun was conventionally represented by a crow, just as the moon was by a hare or toad. In ink-painting the crow's body is also conventionally represented as a single mass of black, and so in Gozan poetry it took on the regular association of a Zen monk in his black robe. The line of crows heading west at sunset thus becomes a group of monks returning to their temple at dusk after a long day of *takuhatsu*, the ritual begging through the community that is a daily part of Zen routine. Gozan poets liked to deliberately further confuse the two mediums by comparing the visual effect of crows against the sky with that of a line of poetry on a scroll, or with drops of ink spattered on paper by a tipsy calligrapher or by children just learning to use brush and ink. In this way each genre adopted practices suggested by the other, interpenetrating one another until the distinction between text and illustration was blurred.

## Periods of Zen Poetry

Three fairly distinct periods can be discerned over the course of the development of medieval Japanese Zen poetry. In the first, lasting from the beginning of the Kamakura period (about 1200) to the schism of the Northern and Southern Courts in 1336, Chinese practices in Zen and poetry were introduced into Japan by Japanese and Chinese monks as part of continental Sung and Yüan dynasty culture. During this period, the establishment of Zen temples in Kamakura and Kyoto laid the foundation for the Gozan system from about 1300. This first period is represented in this volume by the Japanese monks Kakua and Tetsuan Dōshō, and by the Chinese monks Lan-hsi, Wu-hsüeh, and Ming-chi.

The second period began about 1300 with monks like Kokan Shiren (d. 1345), whose succession to the scholastic lines of Chinese monks like

I-shan I-ning marks the beginning of a gradual Japanization of Zen in
Japan. This trend was confirmed by the central role played by Musō
Soseki (d. 1351), the most important figure in the political history of the
Gozan, and reached its highest point with Musō's disciples Gidō Shūshin
(d. 1388) and Zekkai Chūshin (d. 1405). By about 1400 the ways in
which Chinese influences were to be absorbed into Japanese culture were
already more or less determined. This period includes the largest number of monks of the three, seventeen of the twenty-seven whose poetry is
included in this volume.

The third period, which lasted from about 1400–1500, in which we
find many of the most important developments in the medieval Japanese
art-forms, saw also the gradual fossilization of the Gozan system of Zen
temples under the weakening rule of the Ashikaga shoguns. At the same
time that Zen training within the Gozan was giving way to scholarship—
"Zen robes changing to Confucian gowns," as one monk put it—the
Gozan was slowly abdicating its role as the major channel of Chinese
culture into Japan and mediator between the worlds of the Zen monks,
the warrior rulers, and the court nobility. This role was taken over
instead by a new class of cultural arbiters, the *dōbōshū* or "companions
to the shogun" under whose skillful guidance and connoisseurship a new
synthesis of cultural materials was to result in an entirely new Japanese
aesthetic.

The curve that marks the descent of the Gozan in the political and
cultural life of Japan meets that tracing the ascent of the "companions"
in the half-century between 1420 and 1470. With the outbreak of the
Ōnin Civil War in 1467, the Gozan was dispersed and its political and
cultural role brought effectively to an end. Of the monks represented
here who lived during this last period, Kōzei Ryūha, Kisei Reigen and
Keijo Shūrin are the last great flowering of the mainstream Gozan culture, and Nankō Sōgan and Banri Shūkyū that of its more eccentric
constituents.

The poems in this book are arranged into groups that reflect something
of the variety of experience encountered by Zen monks over the course of a
lifetime spent in the world of the Gozan temples. Each section is prefaced
by a brief discussion of the issues raised by the poetry. It is hoped that this
method of organization will permit the reader to understand the poems in
the context of the monks' lives and daily routine. Biographical material on
each poet can be found in the short biographies at the end of the book. One
monk is conspicuous by his absence: the famous, perhaps infamous, Ikkyū
Sōjun (1394–1481), whose life and work, not theoretically a part of the
Gozan per se, are detailed elsewhere.[6]

---

[6] See James Sanford, *Zen Man Ikkyū* (Chico: Scholars Press, 1981), and Sonja Arntzen,
*Ikkyū and the Crazy Cloud Anthology* (Tokyo: University of Tokyo Press, 1984).

# Bibliographical Note

The poems translated here are selected from the enormous body of poetry written by Japanese Rinzai Zen monks from 1200–1500. Their writings have been given the general designation of *Gozan bungaku* or "literature of the Five Mountains." The writings of these monks, especially their official and private diaries, have long been recognized as source materials of considerable importance in medieval history. Their poetry, however, neither part of the literary tradition of the Chinese mainland although it was written in Chinese, nor for this same reason considered in the mainstream of Japanese literature properly speaking, has until recently attracted relatively little notice. The poetry collections of the Zen monks have been made widely available in printed form only in the last half-century, beginning with the appearance of some forty of these collections in *Zoku Gunsho Ruijū* in 1926. This number was expanded to sixty-five with the publication of Uemura Kankō's *Gozan Bungaku Zenshū* in 1936, and to eighty-nine with Tamamura Takeji's *Gozan Bungaku Shinshū* in 1967–72. These three collections account among them for a great deal of the most important poetry written by the medieval Zen monks, but the greater part still remains in manuscripts awaiting appearance in print.

# POEMS

# 1. Doctrine

Some medieval Zen poetry can be called doctrinal in orientation in that it deals with obviously "religious" material. Poems of this sort may make use of specifically Zen jargon, or refer clearly to well-known kōans in their wording or title. These poems are still far removed from the *gātha* or "hymn," the awkward, clumsy expositions of faith or doctrine that usually precede more imagistic poetry at the end of the collected deeds and sayings of the Zen masters.

---

## WRITTEN TO REVEAL MY ENLIGHTENMENT TO MY TEACHER

KAKUA, ZZ 2/2/10: 144b

1

Meaning to get away from the intellectualization and avoid word-traps,
I sailed across the sea to search for the "transmission beyond the
    teachings,"
Went on pilgrimages till my sandals broke—
And found water in the clear stream, the moon in the sky.

2

I cleared away the creeping vines of intellectualization,
Lopped and mowed right through the world of illusion
Till the light of the moon behind my brain broke through to the Great
    Void—
Now each and every age revolves around this moment.

## POEM ON THE KŌAN "JŌSHŪ'S DOG"

LAN-HSI TAO-LUNG, *BZ* 95:88

My snow-white blade relies on heaven's strength;
What is difficult is easy if one sees with eyes of truth.
Ignore the peril to your own lives and draw near—
The world is strewn with skulls in the cold!

> *The poem might not seem to have much to do with the famous
> kōan "Jōshū's Dog" (Mumonkan, case 1) in which the Chinese
> monk Ch'ao-chou (Jōshū, 778–897), asked whether or not a dog
> has Buddha-nature, replied "Mu!" The answer is neither an
> affirmation nor a denial, but an utterance that rejects entirely
> the duality implied by the question. Mumon's own poem on the
> case, however, contains the lines*
>
> > *The moment you deal with 'has' or 'hasn't'
> > You lose your life and perish!*
>
> *Such poems about "dharma battle," the give-and-take between
> two Zen monks, are frequently full of the imagery of weaponry
> and death.*


## WEI-SHAN WAS ATTENDING PAI-CHANG AT HIS LODGING: CHANG TOLD HIM TO SEE IF THERE WAS FIRE IN THE HEARTH OR NOT

LAN-HSI TAO-LUNG, *BZ* 95:88

A lonely river bank, a fishing boat draws near;
Snowy mallows and frosty reeds, sere in the cold.
Who says there's no bait on the end of my pole?
I hooked this golden-scaled fish with no trouble!

> *Wei-shan Ling-yu (771–853) was a disciple of Pai-chang
> Huai-hai (749–814). The poem alludes to a story in the Ching-te
> ch'uan-teng lu (TD, 51:264b): One day Wei-shan was attending
> Pai-chang. . . . Pai-chang said, "Go poke the hearth and see if
> there is any fire." Wei-shan poked the hearth, but there wasn't
> any. Pai-chang rose and, poking more deeply himself, found a
> small coal and showed it to Wei-shan, saying, "I thought you
> said there wasn't any?" Wei-shan was suddenly enlightened.*
>
> > *This poem is among the very first Zen poems in Japan to
> make use of imagery that appears to be entirely poetic, in this
> case the first two lines. The poet seems to say that beneath the
> apparently dead cold winter scene there lies a spark of Zen
> awareness. The last two lines contain the common reference to
> the poem as "bait" used to "hook" the reader's attention.*

## TO A PILGRIM WHO REQUESTED A POEM

WU-HSÜEH TSU-YÜAN, *BZ* 95:349

The Buddha is just an old monk in the Western Heaven—
Is that something to look so hard for day and night?
It's *you* who are the Buddha, but you just won't see—
Why go riding on an ox to search for an ox?!

> *The ox, especially as it figured as the well-known subject of
> poetry and art in the "Ten Ox-herding Pictures," was a symbol
> of the search for enlightenment. The first of the ten pictures
> shows the seeker of enlightenment at the earliest stage of his
> journey, setting off to look for an ox while riding on one—
> unawares, that is, that Buddhahood is already within him.*

## TWENTY-EIGHT SONGS OF THE WAY, AT WHITE CLOUD HERMITAGE—NUMBER NINE

WU-HSÜEH TSU-YÜAN, *BZ* 95:188

A thousand mountains, wind and snow, stop me in my lonely tracks;
Turning my head to the western sky, the road a dead end,
I recall the distant event of Bodhidharma's arrival in China—
An old monkey howls from the highest peak.

> *The third line reads literally, "I recall the distant event of the
> P'u-t'ung era"—that is, the twenty-first day of the ninth month
> of the seventh year of the P'u-t'ung reign-era of Emperor Wu-ti
> of the Liang dynasty (526), a traditional date of Bodhidharma's
> arrival in China.*

## PUTTING ONE FOOT AFTER THE OTHER IS TO PRACTICE THE WAY

MUSŌ SOSEKI, *FGS* 2053

*Furusato to*               At those times
*Sadamuru kata no*          When I cannot decide the way
*Naki toki wa*              Back where I came from,
*Izuku ni yuku mo*          Anywhere I go
*Ieji narikeri.*           Becomes the road home.

RHYMING WITH FIVE POEMS ON A COLD NIGHT

RYŪSHŪ SHŪTAKU, *GBZS* II: 1176

The mice jostling the lamp stand, squeaking and gibbering,
Remind me of the story of Tou-tzu crying "Oil! Oil!"
Rush mat on bamboo platform, I sit through the night,
Unaware that my whole body is running with cold sweat.

> *One day the monk Ch'ao-chou (Jōshū) met a man on the road
> and asked, "Aren't you the abbot Tou-tzu?" Tou-tzu replied, "I
> beg for a coin for tea and salt." Ch'ao-chou said nothing. He
> arrived first at the temple and sat down. Tou-tzu returned
> carrying a jug of oil. Ch'ao-chou said, "I'd heard that Tou-tzu
> lived here, but I only find an oil-seller." Tou-tzu replied, "You
> only see an oil-seller but don't recognize Tou-tzu." "Then who is
> Tou-tzu?" Tou-tzu replied, "Oil! Oil!" (The Chinese is "yu! yu!,"
> also an onomatopoeia for the squeaking of mice.)*
>
> TD 51:319a

IN RESPONSE TO A REQUEST TO
"EXPLAIN THE SECRET TEACHING"

GIDŌ SHŪSHIN, *GBZS* II:1435–36 [560]

If I explained aloud, then it wouldn't be a true explanation,
And if I transmitted it on paper, then where would be the secret?
At a western window on a rainy autumn night,
White hair in the guttering lamplight, asleep facing the bed. . . .

> *Hekiganroku, case 17: A monk asked the Zen Master Kyōrin
> "What is the meaning of Bodhidharma's coming from the
> west?" Kyōrin replied, "Sitting long and getting tired."*

## POEM ON LIVING IN DAIYŪJI TEMPLE (4)

NANKŌ SŌGAN, *GBSS* VI:262

Wind rattles a sour gourd against the wall;
Finally waking from a lingering dream only as the sun sets,
I brew tea over an iron grill, drink three cups—
Beyond this, what is there to say but *mu*!

> The phrase *"sour gourd"* has been variously interpreted as
> referring to the monk's reclusiveness and his shaven head. Mu is
> the utterance that rejects any attempts at making distinctions;
> see the note on the kōan *"Jōshū's Dog"* in the Mumonkan
> (p. 24).

## BELL COLORS

KEIJO SHŪRIN, *GBZS* IV:165

In spring temples, the bell sounds dividing day and night
Are seen by the ear and heard by the eye,
Colors from beyond the sky dyeing everything in two—
Purple in the sunset clouds, red in the dawn.

> The poem is an elaborate metaphysical exploration based on the
> play of meaning of the words shiki *(color; illusory sense-derived
> distinctions of the phenomenal world)* and kū *(sky; emptiness,
> void, non-form)* as they occur in the phrase from the Pra-
> jñāpāramitā Hridāya Sūtra: shiki soku ze kū *('colors are the sky';
> 'the illusory, sense-derived distinctions of the phenomenal world
> made by men are actually empty non-form'). The poet says that
> it is the dawn bell that turns the east red, the dusk bell that
> turns the west purple.*

*Calligraphy by Musō Soseki*

## 2. Meditation and Daily Practice

Meditation was an important part of a Zen monk's life. Many famous Zen stories tell us, however, that because Zen does not make discriminations among things, no one part of life could be more important than any other. Thus, eating, washing one's bowl, going to the bathroom, sleeping, working in the garden—everything one did was Zen.

Still, it is clear from the enormous numbers of poems written on the subject that *zazen* or seated meditation was unquestionably the most demanding of all activities. Physical discomfort is almost never mentioned; presumably Zen monks were accustomed to the physical strain of sitting for long hours in the "lotus" position, each foot resting on its opposite thigh, back erect, nose in line with navel. What took its toll was the mental strain of having to sit this way for years on end with little apparent result. Enlightenment may have been a very personal affair, but monks were always aware not only of the example set by the Buddha, but by their neighbor on the next mat as well. The ability or inability to sit and meditate long hours and concomitant success or failure in attaining enlightenment is the subject of the following poems.

The one day of the year on which these feelings were most intense was Rōhatsu, the eighth day of the twelfth month of the lunar calendar, the day on which the Buddha attained enlightenment. It is the final day of the intensive winter meditation (*sesshin*) during which Zen monks attempt to follow the Buddha's example. Poems composed on this occasion are full of hope and striving, and usually end in temporary defeat as yet one more year goes by without enlightenment.

*Calligraphy by Ōsen Keisan*

## MISCELLANEOUS POEMS FROM MY LAIR

BETSUGEN ENSHI, *GBZS* 1:758

1

Old rat as usual stealing oil from my lamp,
With squeaking screeches leaps about, poking holes in the walls;
And I as usual grab the broom and hurl it through the dark—
If I ever hit him they can put down one more rat-soul for the Western
    Heaven!

2

Dreams of rivers and lakes broken, I sit at midnight in the meditation
    hall;
From empty steps come the steady sounds of long summer rains:
Blink, blonk—the temple roof leaks everywhere,
And every drop stabs clear into my guts.

3

By now I'd be the old dragon rock of Mt. Lu,
White-bearded, grizzle-haired, stern-visaged—
But the temple gate wasn't firmly locked,
And someone's come to pass the time chitchatting. . . .

4

Yakkety-yak: "The textbook's inane, can't you see that?
Stupid business, this facing a wall—I'm worn out from the effort."
I make a deep basket of my sleeves, keep my tongue to myself—
When I open *my* mouth it'll be at mealtime!

5

A myriad trees sway in the wind, yellow leaves flutter down;
The cold color of mountains all around, I don't open my gate:
Someone once planted these cedars in the garden
Just to keep half a day's sunshine from these thatched eaves.

NIGHT MEDITATION

BETSUGEN ENSHI, *GBZS* I:767

Our fate is fixed in heaven before we're born:
Nothing accidental about poverty or success, sinking or swimming;
Counting on my fingers, I reckon back the days and months,
In my mind's eye wander over landscapes of times gone by;
Three thousand strands of white hair in the autumn wind,
Fifty years of guttering lamps in the night rain;
Leaning against the wall, I often think on things of then and now—
With one sound, new geese cross the chilly skies.


SHOWN TO A VILLAGE MONK

JAKUSHITSU GENKŌ, *TD* 81:105b

A monk's come knocking on my brushwood gate,
Wanting to discuss weighty matters of great Zen import:
Excuse this mountain priest, too lazy to open his mouth—
But warblers are singing all over the blossom-strewn village.

> *It is interesting to compare* Man'yōshū 1437 *by* Ōtomo no Ta-
> bito, *which links the* "flower-strewn village" (hanachiruzato)
> *with the* hototogisu ("cuckoo") *rather than the* uguisu ("warbler")
> *of Jakushitsu's poem:*

|  |  |
|---|---|
| Tachibana no | *The days are many* |
| Hanachiruzato no | *When I, like the cuckoo* |
| Hototogisu | *In the village* |
| Kataomoshitsutsu | *Strewn with orange blossoms,* |
| Naku hi shi zo ōku. | *Cry for unrequited love.* |

## SNOW ON RŌHATSU

JAKUSHITSU GENKŌ, *TD* 81:104c

This is the morning that Shakyamuni became the Buddha,
And here this disaster has befallen man and heaven!
Let's go find a spark of fire,
Burn some dry kindling, watch the snow, and sleep.

> *This poem, typical of those written on the eighth day of the twelfth month celebrating the end of the winter intensive meditation period, uses a kind of code language that seems to say the opposite of what it means. The "disaster" is not the snow, but the fact that the poet has failed once again to achieve enlightenment and become a Buddha. The "spark of fire" is the tiny, flickering germ of enlightenment which needs to be fueled and fanned into the real thing. "Sleep," as always in Zen poems, means meditation.*

## THE PATH TO BUDDHAHOOD

SESSON YŪBAI, *GBSS* III:752

1

The snow piled on this empty mountain has frozen the gate shut,
But in the night cold the garden plum-trees burgeon with returning
    spring;
The Moon down, Orion stretches across the sky, people silent and still—
Lying awake, I hear a lone dog howl outside the village.

2

After six years on this snowy peak enduring hunger and cold,
I saw a bright star appear in a blinding flash;
Like molten iron it enclosed the mountain top—
Gautama with that one blunder cast my Buddhahood in doubt.

> *Compare the second poem with "The Road to Buddhahood" by Musō Soseki, p. 38.*

*"Returning, hoe on shoulder, with the setting sun"*

## STAYING AT FA-WANG TEMPLE

SESSON YŪBAI, *GBZS* I:561; *GBSS* III:899

Ice invades the stone runnels, harshens the spring's sound,
Wind rattles bamboos against the window and the moonlight shivers;
Fire dead, ashes cold, a chill comes through the door—
An old monk rises from his meditation, incense just gone out.

## IMPROMPTU

JAKUSHITSU GENKŌ, *TD* 81:105a

All my life I had no great love for high-flown talk—
So lazy, all I craved was sweet, dark sleep,
But a rat's stealthy gnawing sounded at the foot of my bed,
Till the sun pierced the sparse bamboos to shine on the western eaves.

## THE PATH TO BUDDHAHOOD

RYŪSEN REISAI, *GBZS* I:622

Ever since he was young the mountain priest has indulged himself
With the richness of sleeping life away in the woods,
His dreams interrupted only by the mountain light through the
    vine-covered window,
Never knowing the bell has rung, the cocks have crowed.

## ONE OF HEAVEN'S FOLK

RYŪSEN REISAI, *GBZS*, I:630

The sun in the sky is another sojourner through this world
Who feels nothing, never strays, never early or late;
And who is this, neither samurai, farmer, artisan nor merchant,
Returning, hoe on shoulder, with the setting sun?

> *The monk falls into none of the four social classes defined by Confucian ideology, but is rather one of the phenomena of nature.*

## PUTTING THE GARDEN BACK IN ORDER

RYŪSEN REISAI, *GBZS* I:618

Behind the temple, in an overgrown patch I've spaded up,
Vegetables now turn their green toward the hoe;
I won't disobey the rule that Zen monks be productive—
Just one more bald fellow for the official tax-rolls.

## SUMMER NIGHT

KOKAN SHIREN, *GBZS* I:74

To escape the heat I sleep upstairs
Where a slight cool grows in the night:
A frog's croak echoes in a stone basin,
Moonlight casts patterns through bamboo blinds;
I accept every sound and sight that's offered,
The more detached, the more I hear and see;
A time of night I am so truly still
I no longer notice the mosquitoes buzzing round my ears.

## IMPROMPTU POEM (13)

KOKAN SHIREN, *GBZS* I:105

Ricebowl washed clean, I've nothing else to do
But sit idly on my lonely mat
Enjoying the sun through the south window, bright and warm—
I really ought to take advantage of this morning's mood
    To work on my annotations to
       The Laṅkāvatāra Sutra. . . .

> *The Sutra mentioned here is one of the very few Buddhist writings used by the Zen sect, as much because of the legend that Bodhidharma passed it personally to his disciple Hui-k'o, the second Zen Patriarch, as for its abstruse teachings.*

## SITTING IN MEDITATION

BETSUGEN ENSHI, *GBZS* I:755

Mountain temple rainy, dark and gloomy all day,
Plums still half yellow, half green;
On my lone mat, still and quiet, deep in meditation,
I don't let birds and blossoms into my garden by the gate.

## IMPROMPTU POEM

MUSŌ SOSEKI, *TD* 80:480c

Autumn's colors dropping from branches in masses of falling leaves,
Cold clouds bringing rain into the crannies of the mountains:
Everyone was born with the same sort of eyes—
Why do *mine* keep seeing things as Zen kōans?

> *Muso's* waka *poem "Enjoying the evening cool" similarly bleaches
> the landscape of "color"—always a highly charged term in Zen
> metaphysics. In the Chinese poem above and the* waka *below, the
> term assumes the significance of the illusory manifold distinc-
> tions that comprise the phenomenal world, reduced by the poet's
> eye to a universal monochrome:*

| | |
|---|---|
| Kurenu yori | *The color of the evening* |
| Yūbe no iro wa | *Has departed before* |
| Sakidachite | *The red of the setting sun:* |
| Kikage suzushiki | *In the trees' shade, cool* |
| Tanikawa no mizu. | *Water of the valley stream.* |

Mūso Soseki, *ST* V:162:42; *GSRJ* 15:361b

## THE ROAD TO BUDDHAHOOD

MUSŌ SOSEKI, *TD* 80:476c

I sat freezing for six years like a snake in bamboo,
Till ice and snow began to seem my style of Zen;
Last night I saw the empty sky burst open,
And rose alarmed, bright stars in my eyes.

> *Musō's Collected Sayings (TS 80:484c) records his experience of
> false enlightenment in 1304 at the age of 30:*
>
> > One night as the Master was sitting by the hearth, sparks
> > suddenly left the fire and began to burn in the middle of
> > the sky, flashing like lightning. His eyes were dazzled and
> > his chest was bursting. The next day he again saw the sun
> > shining on the clumps of bamboo outside the window, their
> > intertwined shadows swaying in the wind.
>
> *The Chinese poem may be compared with Musō's* waka *poem,
> "Untitled":*

| | |
|---|---|
| Satori tote | *It is precisely the fact* |
| Tsune ni wa kawaru | *That an ever-changing mind* |
| Kokoro koso | *Thinks it is enlightened* |
| Mayoi no naka no | *That reveals it has strayed* |
| Mayoi narikere. | *From the wrong path to one even* |
| | *more wrong.* |

*GSRJ* XV:363a; *ST* V:164:74

## UNTITLED

KŌHŌ KENNICHI, *FGS* 2065

| | |
|---|---|
| *Yo mo sugara* | If you would inquire |
| *Kokoro no yukue* | Of my heart's whereabouts |
| *Tazunereba* | Throughout the night: |
| *Kinō no sora ni* | Where are the traces of birds' flight |
| *Tobu tori no ato.* | Through yesterday's sky? |

## SWEEPING LEAVES

RYŪSHŪ SHŪTAKU, *GBZS* II:1173 [296]

Lacking cash to buy firewood,
I sweep up leaves from the road in front,
Each one as valuable as gold;
Piled up like gorgeous red brocades,
I covet them greedily for warming my knees,
And to bring some comfort to my cold heart:
I'll take them back to burn in the hearth while I sit in meditation,
And return to listening to the rain dripping on the steps.

> *One scholar has interpreted this poem to mean that the monk is*
> *sweeping the leaves up to sell for cash. The usual conceit, how-*
> *ever, is that a Zen monk burns leaves fallen from the trees in*
> *autumn because his chosen poverty does not permit him to buy*
> *firewood, and his Zen philosophy makes him see the leaves'*
> *value only in their simple utility, not in the illusory "color"*
> *which others find so appealing. See for example Keijo Shūrin's*
> *"Crimson Maples Beyond the Bamboos" (p. 51).*

## SPRING RAIN, IDLE THOUGHTS

RYŪSHŪ SHŪTAKU, *GBZS* II:1175 [299]

Quitely I watch spring clouds grow in the vast sky,
Green mountains and white hair on opposite sides of slatted bamboo
    blinds;
A myriad miles of heaven and earth rain with white blossoms
And all of them are falling in one Zen monk's eyes.

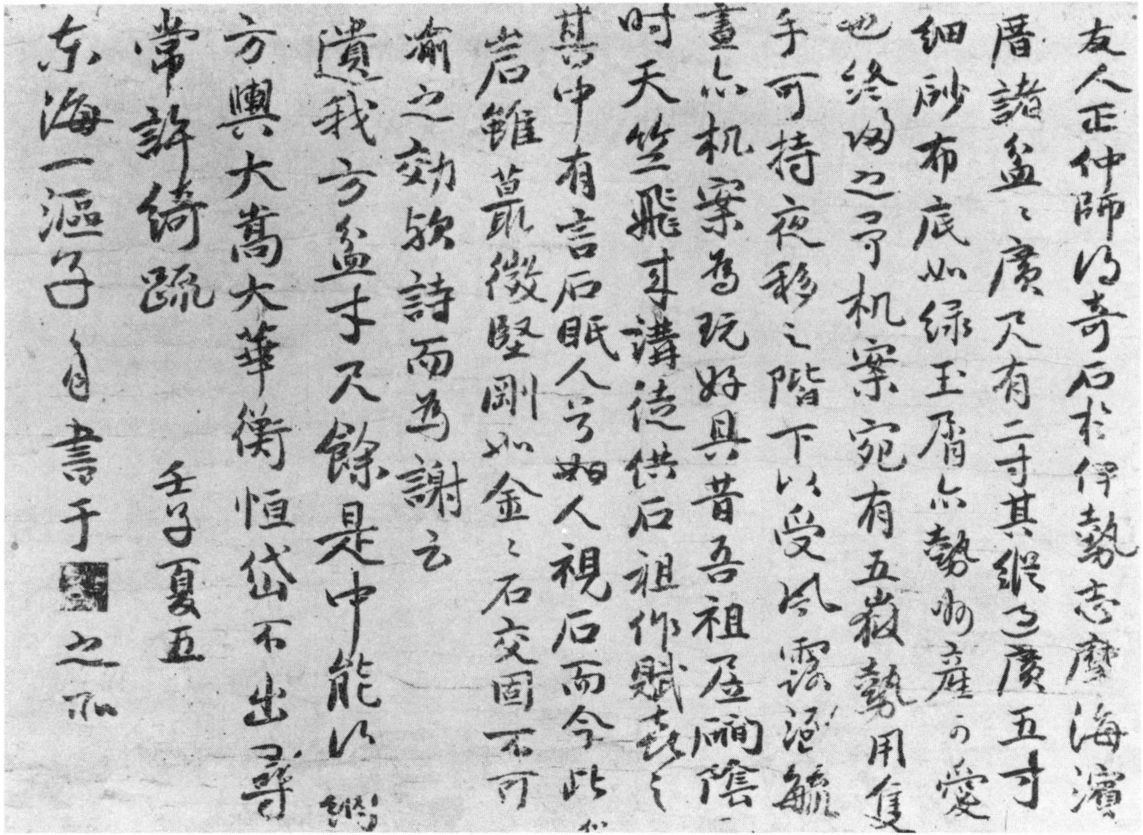

*Calligraphy by Chūgan Engetsu*

## AT FUJIGAYATSU: WRITING MY THOUGHTS

CHŪGAN ENGETSU, *GBZS* II:910 [34]; *GBSS* IV:333

1

Murky air off the sea brings spring gloom
Like pestilential fog from the barbaric south;
I wake reluctantly from a troubled sleep, head heavy with cobwebs,
Half sober, half drunk, clutching the cold quilt.

2

The day drags on forever with rain that never ends;
I keep dozing off and starting awake again:
"Brew some tea," "Change the water"—I keep pestering the boy,
Lean on the desk and open a book to clear away this mood.

3

I dreamed I was discussing ancient literature with Confucius and
    Mencius:
They both held that the affairs of this world were but floating clouds;
Having dashed madly in all directions, I now lurk here in the shadows of
    Wisteria Valley,
Heaven and earth emptied of their last valiant steed.

4

A single grain of clarity that shone in the night like a pearl—
Covered with dust and dirt and smeared with sticky mud so long,
The God of the Sea, unable to recognize it for what it is,
Has given it to the dung-beetles to add to the balls they roll.

5

These eight, nine years since I returned from China,
I've worn out my soul trying to raise a crop on rocks:
Scorched sprouts, rotted plants—what use are they?
Best to stop tilling and go back to sleep.

## POEM WHILE LIVING AT THE LING-CHIANG MOUNTAIN TEMPLE

TESSHŪ TOKUSAI, *GBZS* II:1289 [413]

Movement and stillness: both are part of the same principle,
Emotions of this dusty world are not as important as the Way,
So I endure this thin paper robe until the dawn bell,
While pomegranate leaves and mulberry branches dance in the north
    wind.

## LISTENING TO THE PINES

TESSHŪ TOKUSAI, *GBZS* II:1286 [410]

A raging wind shuddering through the high trees with year-end cold,
Raises the sound of ocean waves a thousand feet high,
A sound pitched high beyond this dusty world—
The mind never hears with the clarity of the ear.

> *The last line inverts the usual Zen conceit that perceiving with*
> *the mind is superior to perceiving with the senses.*

## COLD NIGHT: SENT TO TEKIAN

TESSHŪ TOKUSAI, *GBZS* II:1285 [409]

The moon illuminates a thousand peaks with the brilliance of daylight,
The sound of the bell falls on my pillow of old friends' poems;
In my thin monk's robes, unafraid of the frost's harshness,
I rise, roll up the thin blinds, sit in the depths of the night.

## DESULTORY POEM

CHŪGAN ENGETSU, *GBZS* II:902

The older I get, the more narrowly I look upon the world, and the more
    I detest affectation:
In fact, every now and again, I actually *like* the pretty things of the
    world!
Giving in to my true nature, I open the window onto the small pond,
And, chin on fist, gaze into the infinity beyond:
Blown by the breeze, butterflies flit through sweet-smelling grasses,
Everywhere dragonflies rest on lotus-blossoms—
If the "cold and tasteless" in these seem so sweet to me,
What am I doing living in a temple?

> *On the technical term "cold and tasteless," see Introduction,*
> *p. 10.*

## TWO POEMS RHYMING WITH BETSUGEN ENSHI'S

CHŪGAN ENGETSU, *GBZS* II:902

### 1

The temple howls on every side, wakening me from my dreams,
As a waning moon sets, brightening the window;
The bark-fiber quilt is cold as iron, not worth clutching—
How can I bear listening to the mountain wind whirling the leaves?

### 2

The hemp robe I wear is torn, not worth fixing,
The leaves for fuel are cold ashes, hard to make red again;
I am forlorn, deceived by those old poets' metaphors—
Maybe I wasn't cut out for their sort of Zen . . . ?

## RHYMING WITH "OPENING THE HEARTH"

KOKEN MYŌKAI, *GBZS* III:2127 [171]

I scrape dead ashes into a pile, sick bones cold,
On the woods full of yellow leaves rain rattles dryly;
No one to play host to, I gather up some leaves again
To be chewed to pieces and made part of the red within the iron ring.

> *In the jargon of Zen, the "iron ring" is the arena in which all
> distinctions are pulverized and made one; its symbol is the
> hearth in which all colors are reduced to the single red of fire.
> "Opening the hearth" at the start of autumn was one of the
> conventional seasonal markers in the Zen temples that came to
> demand an appropriate poem.*

## COMPOSED IN THE RAIN

KOKEN MYŌKAI, *GBZS* III:2117 [161]

All day long, in the sound of rain dripping from the eaves,
I sat patiently, listening with my eyes;
Now I raise the thin blinds onto the western foothills
And the single green of a thousand pines.

## COTTON ROBE

GIDŌ SHŪSHIN, *GBZS* II:1369 [493]

Szechuan brocades, Chiangsu damasks, Fukien gauzes—
Elegance isn't measured by the number of robes one has;
Over and over my seams rip and I sew them up again,
Heat and cold come and go—they don't bother me.

## INSCRIBED ON THE PAVILION OF MOON ON THE WATER: TWO POEMS

GIDŌ SHŪSHIN, *GBZS* II:1355 [479]

1

In the water is a moon gleaming like gold
That I greedily watch at my open window deep into each night;
My sick eyes suddenly cause another to appear—
A monkey's leaped into the blue ripples of my mind!

2

By the light of the moon in the water I sit in meditation,
A wide Palace of Cold soaking into smooth, blue glass;
At midnight I rise, turn suddenly around,
And find the perfect circle of moon in the heart of the ripples.

> *The moon is a symbol of enlightenment, and the perfect round-ness of the full moon used especially to represent certain Tendai ideas. On Gidō's "sick eyes," see his biography, p. 150.*

## BEGINNING OF SPRING: WRITTEN DURING SNOW

GIDŌ SHŪSHIN, *GBZS* II:1391 [515]

I sit firmly on my dried-up mat, thoughts dead as ashes,
When the boy rushes in to announce that spring has returned—
The empty cold smashed to bits, the heavens dance with blossoms
That stir up what I've tried all my futile life to still!

*". . . that old curly-headed fellow,*
*Barefoot, descending his long, steep slope"*

## POEM RHYMING WITH THE MONK SAN'S "TRIP TO KANAZAWA—RECALLING OLD TIMES"

GIDŌ SHŪSHIN, *GBZS* II:1482–83 [606–7]

Miserably cold, the temple before dawn,
Still and lonely, few monks to be seen;
The temple is old, with soot-blackened walls,
The pond overgrown, its surface like folds in a robe;
Incense before the Buddha has burned, gone out, turned cold,
The sermon over, blossoms fly in the rain;
I've reached the point of doing away with happiness and sadness—
A white board door swinging to and fro in the breeze.

## RŌHATSU: TO SHOW TO MY DISCIPLES

GIDŌ SHŪSHIN, *GBZS* II:1490 [614]

The older one gets, the harder it is to achieve Buddhahood;
Ill now, I'm too weary to leave the temple.
But for the rest of you who must make it across,
The ways of the world are more difficult still.
I wake, stars hang low over the doorway,
The sky lightens, snow hugs the gate;
I feel sympathy for that old curly-headed fellow,
Barefoot, descending his long, steep slope.

> *Rōhatsu, the eighth day of the twelfth month, is the day that the Buddha Shakyamuni (frequently referred to as "the curly-headed fellow") attained Buddhahood, and is the final day of the intensive Rōhatsu winter period of meditation during which monks attempt to follow the Buddha's example.*

## INSCRIBED ON A PAINTING SCROLL OF THE WHITE CLOUD MOUNTAIN TEMPLE

ZEKKAI CHŪSHIN, *GBZS* II:1911 [1035]

Built at the foot of green hills in accordance with geomantic divination,
This Zen temple dwells among white clouds
In the forest rill's very deepest spot,
Where monkeys and birds flock to themselves;
The floating mists that come in through the windows are damp,
Fine grasses fragrant and green on the steps;
In the freshness of the morning, daily sutra-reading over,
I sweep the rocks and sit in the regenerating mist.


## KYOTO TEMPLES: FLOWER VIEWING

ZEKKAI CHŪSHIN, *GBZS* II:1934 [1058]

The nobility often come to visit temples near the Imperial Palace,
But for flower viewing I prefer my garden's deep seclusion;
Zen minds do not succumb to spring colors—
Yet in every temple, bamboo blinds are rolled up on their hooks.


## SPRING RAIN

GAKUIN EKATSU, *GBZS* III:2650 [692]

I sit facing the rain in new melancholy, in a room over the wall,
As mist-shrouded trees float gloomily beyond the pale;
Risen from my nap, I'd never know it was a spring day,
Blinds so full of the twilight color of ancient mountains in autumn.

> *The poems by Gakuin are from the period of his stay in China*
> *between 1386 and 1395. Poems about Japan do not usually con-*
> *tain expressions like "room over a wall" (ch'eng-lou, a second-*
> *story room built over a city wall—a sight unknown in Japan), or*
> *"pale"—an attempt to avoid using "wall" in translating* kuo.
> *Since the poet is in another country, the expression "ancient*
> *mountains" (ku shan) can also be interpreted to mean "home-*
> *land temple."*

## READING LAMP

GAKUIN EKATSU, *GBZS* III:2664 [706]

A speck of greenish lamplight, its service over—
Through the years, how many books did it illuminate for me?
But now that I've made my way in the world,
I no longer hear the thin night rains at my still window.

> *In many of his poems, highly charged with Zen ideas, the T'ang poet Po Chü-i referred to the paradox of turning the lamp to the wall the better to hear the rain. The poet seems to say that since he no longer needs to stay up late at night in meditation, he no longer puts away his study of the sutras and turns his lamp to the wall, with the result that he no longer hears the night rain falling.*

## RUNDOWN ROBE

SEIIN SHUNSHŌ, *GBZS* III:2720 [762]

We've been through a lot a years together, grimy with dirt and grease:
So what if it lets in the wind and cold at night?
I've grown partial to the way it hangs, as only a poet could—
Better than a palace robe cut from Chinese cloth!

## POEM WHILE LIVING AT DAIYŪJI TEMPLE (2)

NANKŌ SŌGAN, *GBSS* VI:262

I laugh at my dragon-headed, snake-tailed Zen:
Two years of eating on a patron's hospitality
Like the monkey that dances to a flute in the market south of the
    village—
Black Li's hearth is as full of smoke as Chang San's!

> *The expression "Black Li" is a generic Chinese nickname for any village priest, and Chang San means something like "John Doe."*

## PINES AND GULLS

KEIJO SHŪRIN, *GZBS* IV:79

Wind rolls through the pine branches in my garden,
Rippling the moonlight like waves on a river or lake;
All night long I listen to the wind's sounds, idly hug my quilt,
Wondering whether I dreamed the white gulls or not. . . .

## PAINTING OF PEACH BLOSSOMS ON A WRITING STAND

KISEI REIGEN, *GBSS* II:262

A whole bookcase crowded with volumes—hard to read them all,
No time to peek out at the garden the whole spring night!
But beyond the hedge, the branch of half-open peach blossoms smiles—
He doesn't realize he's madly chanting poems while staring at a closed
     book. . . .

## LISTENING TO SNOW IN THE PLUM TREE

KEIJO SHŪRIN, *GBZS* IV:83

Snow falls on the plum tree with such a soft sound that
On the other side of the window I can't tell (sitting at midnight
In dark fragrance and sparse shadows on a windless night)
If it's the sound of blossoms or of moonlight.

## THE SOUND OF SANDALS

KEIJO SHŪRIN, *GZBS* IV:165

The pale moon may be hazy on the verandas of palace women,
The spring wind gentle and warm in court offices,
But old age brought *my* monk's staff—it wasn't conferred by the court!
The sound of my sandals in the dawn frost would freeze their ears.

## CRIMSON MAPLES BEYOND THE BAMBOOS

KEIJO SHŪRIN, *GBZS* IV:264

Maple trees are renewed by the frosty dawn,
And all around them a spare canopy of green bamboos;
Upstairs, they're writing poems about "regrets for the red leaves,"
But a rustic monk busy sweeping them up for fuel
  wouldn't know about it.

## FISH-OIL LAMP AT A ROADSIDE INN

BANRI SHŪKYŪ, *GBSS* VI:760

Oil squeezed from fish guts makes the lamp burn strange,
A hazy light in a dim room reeking of fish;
Midnight, can't sleep, try to trim the lamp—
And the tiny glow is buried in a real fog.

## STILL A RED-LOOKING SPARK IN THE HEARTH

KEIJO SHŪRIN, *GBZS* IV:174

The dawn bell: wind fans the fire in the drafty hearth,
Cold air whips my mat, finally gets beneath my skin,
But my heart is not yet ash—a tiny speck of crimson
Stirs and dies; there, then gone again.

  *See note, p. 24.*

## THE WAY TO BUDDHAHOOD:
## A POEM WHILE LIGHTING THE INCENSE

GIDŌ SHŪSHIN, *GBZS* II:1428 [552]

Toward dawn the same bright stars return night after night,
On the mountain ranges, winter snows appear every year:
Silly to imagine from these things that Gautama is in any particular
  place—
Like carving nicks on the side of a boat to mark its place in the river!

ON THE NIGHT OF THE TWENTY-FIFTH, THE SIXTH MONTH
OF 1337, A COUPLET CAME TO ME IN A DREAM:
WAKING, I FINISHED THE POEM

JAKUSHITSU GENKŌ, *TD* 81:102a

Life is as illusory as dew, a lightning flash,
In the end just a deceptive dazzle of light;
Events can go swarming past in confusion as they will—
I eat my white rice, watch the green mountains.

# 3. Exhortations and Warnings

These poems were written to urge a pupil on or to warn him from a wrong path. The subjects include admonitions against an attempt to paint a monk's portrait or trying to explain Zen logically, against a Zen monk who would rather be an aristocrat, and, paradoxically, against the writing of poetry itself.

---

## RHYMING WITH A POEM HUMOROUSLY PRESENTED TO THE REGENT

GIDŌ SHŪSHIN, *GBZS* II:1540 [664]

The minor art of poetry isn't worth a coin—
Best just to sit silently in Zen meditation;
Wild words and fancy diction don't cease to violate Buddha's Law
Just because he died two thousand years ago!

> *Among the "Ten Violations" of the Buddhist Law are four that come under the general rubric of "Sins of the Mouth": "wild words" or untruth; "fancy diction" or unnecessarily embellished speech; "slander"; and "hypocrisy." The Buddhist interpretation of non-religious poems, or of any literature that exists for the sake of art, condemns them as "wild words" and "fancy diction."*
>
> *Gidō seems to be suggesting "humorously" to the Regent Nijō Yoshimoto that the two millenia since the Buddha's death have permitted men to find elaborate rationalizations for their continual pursuit of poetry.*

# PRESENTED TO THE PORTRAIT PAINTER DŌRIN

GIDŌ SHŪSHIN, *GBZS* II:1398 [522]

The portrait painter monk Kōsei [Dōrin] passed by my gate and asked if
he could paint a "Portrait of Kūge" [Gidō]. Refusing, I said jokingly,
"This mountain priest's elusive face is like 'blossoms in the air' [*kūge*]—
just as they are revealed they are annihilated. Where do you propose to
begin painting *that*?" The monk laughed, "I'll start with the 'revealing
and annihilating' part." I laughed and wrote this poem in thanks:

There could never be an accurate portrait of "blossoms in the air"—
When the visage is done, it won't be a true likeness;
Put down your brush and look again closely:
It's in the blank space of the background that the figure materializes.


# WRITTEN TO REVEAL MY ENLIGHTENMENT TO MY TEACHER

KAKUA, ZZ 2/2/10: 144b

Raising your fists, shouting, showing off,
Saying "is," saying "isn't" all get you into muddy water;
Always discriminating among things—stop pointing at your
    commentaries!
Nothing comes back but the sound of a flute: la, la, lee. . . .

> *One of the few of Kakua's extant poems, this appears to refer to*
> *an occasion recorded by Kokan Shiren in his* Genkō Shakusho *of*
> *1322: Kakua, invited by Emperor Takakura (1161–1181) to*
> *expound the principles of Zen, merely played the flute in reply.*

## HUMOROUS POEM: WATCHING A CROW BATHE

GIDŌ SHŪSHIN, *GBZS* II:1351 [475]

I've watched you bathe for quite a while, old crow,
And it's going to take some doing to get you white as a gull;
Why not just stay your usual pitch-black self,
And avoid giving the other birds reason to be suspicious?

> *The Zen monk is customarily portrayed in art as a crow because
> of the appearance of his massive black robes. Gidō may have
> been addressing this to a monk who, as was the tendency from
> his day, thought it more elegantly aristocratic to wear brightly
> colored robes.*

## RHYMING WITH A NEW YEAR'S POEM

RYŪSHŪ SHŪTAKU, *GBZS* II:1198 [322]

Three, two, one; one, two, three—
How are *you* ever going to probe the mysteries of Zen?
Spring birds busy on my roof after the rain
Try out some new sounds, tweeting and chirping.

> *This poem is addressed to the poet's pupils, whose attempts at
> answering kōans (Zen parables for meditation) he likens to the
> sounds of young birds learning to chirp.*

## SHOWN TO MY PUPILS

JAKUSHITSU GENKŌ, *TD* 81:104b

To do Zen you've got to be so tough
That body and mind are tempered to beaten iron!
Look at all the Patriarchs who came before—
Which of them ever fooled around like you?!

TO A NEPHEW

JAKUSHITSU GENKŌ, *TD* 81:104c

You must believe the Zen sect doesn't rely on words:
Why do you hang around here? What is it you want?
Straw sandals on your feet! The west wind quickens!
The eighth month already! It's nearly mid-autumn!

## 4. Living in Hermitage

After their initial training in the monasteries of the large metropolitan Rinzai Zen temples was over, monks either were sent or chose to go off to small, remote temples far from the distractions of the urban centers. For some monks this move was politically expedient; for others it was merely a necessary step in the advancement in rank through the temple world that many hoped would end with the abbacy of one of the major Gozan temples in Kamakura or Kyoto. These poems record the experiences of living alone in small mountain retreats, either out of preference or necessity.

---

LIVING IN THE MOUNTAINS

TESSHŪ TOKUSAI, *GBZS* II:1290 [414]

1

To shake off the dust of human ambition
I sit on moss in Zen robes of stillness,
While through the window, in the setting sun of late autumn,
Falling leaves whirl and drop to the stone dais.

2

Old cedars and ancient cypresses impale rosy mists,
Through huge boulders and hanging vines a small path winds;
Even monkeys and cranes won't come to a mountain *this* desolate—
Only the wind-borne cassia pods that fill my thatched hut.

## IN THE SHADOW OF WISTERIA VALLEY:
## MISCELLANEOUS POEMS FROM FUJIGAYATSU

CHŪGAN ENGETSU, *GBZS* II:911 [35]; *GBSS* IV:345

### 1

It's not that I have any deep-seated dislike of visitors—
I just don't like their tramping down half the moss in my garden;
But those who aren't monks and don't know about such feelings
Are surprised when I don't answer their knocking at the gate.

### 2

Moon white, wind clear; filled with autumn thoughts,
Idle in my out-of-the-way temple, small gate left open,
Chanting a poem, I lean on the balustrade, midnight come and gone—
Isn't *someone* in the mood to come visiting tonight?

## DWELLING IN THE MOUNTAINS:
## A POEM RHYMING WITH CH'AN-YÜEH'S (2)

ZEKKAI CHŪSHIN, *GBZS* II:1914 [1038]

I sing and whistle, don't give a hoot for any haughty prince!
Who can keep his head bowed for long under a low ceiling?
Blue seas and purple mountains often appeared in my dreams,
But few would come with me on my rambles through southern clouds
        and lakes.
Misty drizzle from the azure sky dampens my sutra-desk,
Stretches of cold clouds fill the rock escarpments;
Fortunate for me that no one likes the smell of *these* yams—
Following the teachings, I run after vegetable leaves in the creek.

> *"These yams"* alludes to the story of Lai Ts'an, the Chinese her-
> mit who lived by himself on wild yams roasted over dung fires.
> *"Running after vegetable leaves"* refers to the story of the
> Ch'an monk Hsüeh-feng who, having decided to study at a
> certain temple, turned back after seeing cut vegetable leaves
> floating down the stream, certain that such a wasteful place was
> not fit for study. He changed his mind, however, when he saw a
> monk running down the stream chasing after the leaves.

"*Isn't* someone *in the mood to come visiting tonight?*"

## DWELLING IN THE MOUNTAINS:
## A POEM RHYMING WITH CH'AN-YÜEH'S (5)

ZEKKAI CHŪSHIN, *GBZS* II:1915 [1039]

Few people know of this nest hidden in an out-of-the-way spot,
Where the dark green of ivy on ancient trees gleams in the doorway.
Their meal of sweet-smelling grasses over, grey deer sleep;
Having picked all the small pears, white monkeys have scattered.
Washing my robe in creek water, I trouble the clouds' reflections,
Delight in the play of the sunlight on herbs drying from sunny eaves;
The servant lad, unable to comprehend the notion of "permanence in
     change,"
Reproaches me each morning with the thinness of my hair.


## PROTECTING CHRYSANTHEMUMS AFTER A FROST

SEIIN SHUNSHŌ, *GBZS* III:2712 [754]

No need to protect the flowers growing in wild clumps in my temple
     garden—
Even late in the season they can stand many nights of frost;
But recently, with the craze for rare specimens for the fall flower
     competitions,
People's insatiable greed seems to extend even to a monk's hut.


## BAMBOO PAVILION: COOL RAIN

ISHŌ TOKUGAN, *GBSS* II:889

Before the eaves, slender bamboos, a thousand stalks of jade,
Sing, when the cool rains fall, with a rustling sound,
Their feathery green intruding at my desk—
They know there is no purer hidden spot than this.

蓭中有主從君任無主外來俱得珞雲烟眯目山礉齎

榛莽欺人溪澗怒看它本色任菴人揑飛太千坐

一塵自見涯牛聞入海不知住生縱筆萬頭陀休

趙州一世初學一炊夢口身白醿未畉松誰能更言語

方頌持麥抛敚烈燄中嶁種香山芋与莊舊地頀

頭輕篆蓺六林間石上虎吼天風

右雪峯老東山与香山盧頭陀偈書于縹雲窩

*Calligraphy by Zekkai Chūshin*

## TRANSPLANTING ORCHIDS

KŌZEI RYŪHA, *GBSS* VII:174

On a large plot of new land I've cut back thorns and weeds,
Built little supporting frames, made enclosing palings,
Rushed off to pray at the shrine of Ch'u Yüan, their tutelary god—
Growing wise is nowhere near the trouble of growing orchids!

## GYŪKŌ-AN HERMITAGE

GIDŌ SHŪSHIN, *GBZS* II:1464 [588]

Wind wails mournfully in the broken roof as I sit through the long night;
I start suddenly when a gust of rain blows through the forest branches,
And rising, hurry to whet the scythe—
Tomorrow I'm off to cut thatch in the southern hills.

## RHYMING WITH POEMS SENT BY SEVERAL FRIENDS
## TO MY HERMITAGE IN MIURA

MUSŌ SOSEKI, *TD* 80:477a

1

Warped wood, never lumber for great mansions,
Could scarcely expect to be used in a noble house;
But, flung to this faraway fishing village,
It can help prop up the fishermen's piers.

2

In my pot nothing but the wind's deep moan,
For company only a staff of wisteria vine;
Last night we chatted and laughed till all hours—
The empty sky listened with a cold heart.

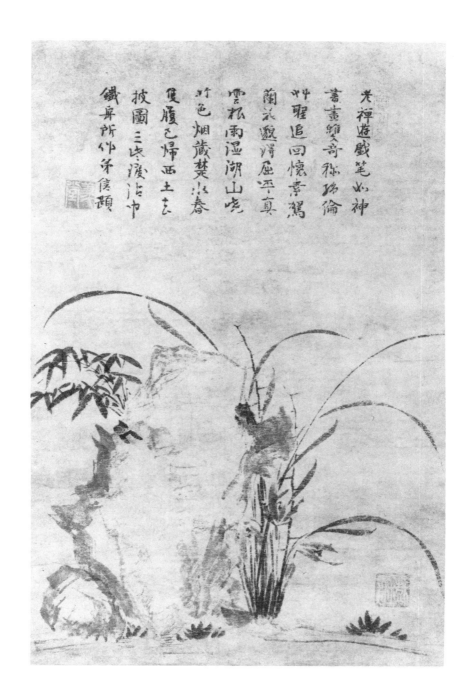

*"Growing wise is nowhere near the trouble of growing orchids!"*

## I HID AWAY AT THE KEIZAN MOUNTAIN TEMPLE IN MINO

MUSŌ SOSEKI, *GSRJ* XV:362b

Though so deep in the mountains there was not even a real road of any sort to the spot, much to my annoyance people kept calling to study Zen with me:

| | |
|---|---|
| *Yo no usa ni* | It would be merciful of people |
| *Kaetaru yama no* | Not to come calling and disturb |
| *Sabishisa o* | The loneliness of these mountains |
| *Towanu zo hito no* | To which I have returned |
| *Nasakenarikeru.* | From the sorrows of the world. |

> In 1311 Musō built a retreat he named Ryūsan-an. Hounded by would-be students, he abandoned the retreat in 1312 to live at the temple of his teacher Kōhō Kennichi, Jōkyoji in the province of Kai. In 1313 Musō left for Nagaseyama in Mino and lodged at Eihōji (the mountain designation of which was Kokeizan or "Tiger Valley Mountain"), again in order to escape the students who came to seek him out. The waka poem above echoes a well-known poem by the priest Saigyō:

| | |
|---|---|
| Tou hito mo | *If it were not for the loneliness* |
| Omoitaetaru | *Of this mountain village* |
| Yamazato no | *Where people have given up* |
| Sabishisa nakuba | *calling on me,* |
| Sumiukaramashi | *It would probably be* |
| | *Wretched to live here.* |

## WRITTEN WHILE VISITING

MUSŌ SOSEKI, *TD* 80:476c

A drifter all my life, I never saved a thing:
Clouds in the mountains, moon in the creek for carpets,
East to west I trod this narrow track for nothing—
It wasn't in the dwellings along the way.

> Compare this poem in Chinese with Musō's waka poem entitled "Abandoning the Hermitage I was living in that I had built in Shimizu in Mino":

| | |
|---|---|
| Ikutabi ka | *How many times* |
| Kakusumi sutete | *Have I left abandoned,* |
| Idetsuramu | *Living hidden away like this,* |
| Sadamenaki yo ni | *A temporary dwelling built* |
| Musubu kariio. | *In an uncertain world?* |

FGS 1783

## UNTITLED

KŌHŌ KENNICHI, *FGS* 1747

| | |
|---|---|
| *Ware dani mo* | The white clouds |
| *Sebashi to omou* | On the mountain-tops |
| *Kusa no io ni* | Poke halfway into this thatched hut |
| *Nakaba sashiiru* | I had thought too cramped |
| *Mine no shiragumo.* | Even for myself. |

## RHYMING WITH THE PRIEST TS'AO-AN'S POEM "LIVING IN THE MOUNTAINS" (7)

BETSUGEN ENSHI, *GBZS* I:749

Cranes in the wilderness, lonely clouds—their destination is uncertain:
Where in this world am I to address my deepest thoughts?
Forest trees in serried ranks ascend the cliff walls,
Like a series of brush strokes, hills and peaks arrayed out to the horizon;
My mind brims with Zen clear as water,
Old bones jut angularly thin as kindling;
Fame is nothing one can keep for long—
A hundred years of light and dark before we reach our end.

## TWENTY-EIGHT SONGS OF THE WAY AT WHITE CLOUD HERMITAGE (22)

WU-HSÜEH TSU-YÜAN, *BZ* 95:188

Wild mountain potatoes come up big as fists,
So I'm not scared of the harsh winter that cuts through my patched
    robes;
Fire's gone cold deep in the clouds, no word from outside:
The yellow leaves can go ahead and fill the steps.

## LIVING IN THE MOUNTAINS (1)

TETSUAN DŌSHŌ, *GBZS* I:371

Too much happens here where nothing should at all:
A thatched hut is not supposed to be a busy place.
But mountain birds come to flee the evening rain in these dense woods,
Stream oysters gleam in morning light in the clear waters,
Clouds drip patterns of slippery moss on stone beds,
Spring brings tea's fragrance to water in an earthenware crock:
This floating world is just a tune whistled on a sword hilt—
Fame and fortune have forgotten all about me.

> *The "tune whistled on a sword hilt," a phrase from the Chinese
> Taoist philosopher Chuang Tzu, provides a nice touch of futility
> to all the busy activities of man and nature.*

## LIVING IN THE MOUNTAINS (2)

TETSUAN DŌSHŌ, *GBZS* I:372

An empty mountain has no place for worldly entanglements,
The pure sound of a bell no right or wrong:
Water falls in the scars of creeks where icy bones have broken,
Moons grow in corners of rooms as tree shadows shift,
Incense hovers, printing antique characters from a lone censer,
While I prune back proliferating lines of poetry from recent drafts;
To the world this life tastes cold and sour—I find it pleasingly stark,
But only the old cranes and wild monkeys know.

> *The Sōtō Zen monk Dōgen Kigen (1200–1253) is said to have
> refused the honor of a purple robe bestowed upon him by
> Emperor Go-Saga two times, then finally yielded to the
> Emperor's wish but refused to wear it. On this occasion he
> wrote the following poem:*
>
> > *Though the valley below Eiheiji is not deep,*
> > *I am profoundly honored to receive the Imperial
> >     Command,*
> > *But I would be laughed at by monkeys and cranes*
> > *If an old monk wore a purple robe!*
>
> *[See Joseph Kitagawa,* Religion in Japanese History *(New York:
> Columbia University Press, 1966) 127 and note 97].*

RHYMING WITH THE PRIEST TS'AO-AN'S POEM
"LIVING IN THE MOUNTAINS" (9)

BETSUGEN ENSHI, *GBZS* I:749

1

In this wretched, thatched-roof hut I have my secret fun:
Lounge around, sleep, whatever suits my fancy,
And laugh at preachers who come from all around
With their sneaky spiels, fervent bellows, wild gesticulations.

2

All the hundred thousand Buddhas are just dust in my eyes,
Those folks up there in heaven—they're no neighbors of mine;
I keep my fire going with kindling that smokes, flares up, goes out—
How can I leave any here for those to come after?

## 5. Festivals and Holidays

The Gozan monks observed the important seasonal markers of the Chinese lunar calendar, as all Japanese had since its adoption in 645. They followed the custom of inaugurating a new writing-brush on the New Year by writing an appropriate poem, and celebrated especially the Chinese festivals that called for writing poetry; among the best known were the festivals of the third day of the third month and the ninth day of the ninth month. Because they had fewer poetic associations, the more popular festivals of the fifth day of the fifth month (*tango no sekku*), the "Boy's Festival" of today, and the seventh day of the seventh month or "*Tanabata*" festival are mentioned less often. The poets enjoyed exploring the paradoxes of ancient Chinese festivals as they were observed in Japan, where the traditional Chinese herbs often could not be obtained. The rowdy and raucous crowds thronging the streets of the great cities are frequently contrasted to the solitary monk seated quietly in meditation inside his temple, attempting to be oblivious to it all but having little success.

---

FIRST WRITING OF THE YEAR: NEW YEAR'S DAY, 1489

BANRI SHŪKYŪ, *GBSS* VI:756

From the mouth of the bay spring wind churns waves a frothy green,
In the traveler's room a rooster welcomes in the gloomy dawn;
Hurriedly I grind some ink to test my writing-brush:
Poetry is my *Prajñāpāramitā Sūtra*.

## ON A FAN

KEIJO SHŪRIN, *GBZS* IV:130

In country houses the saké is hot, everyone dead drunk:
Couldn't have had more fun in the days of the Sage Emperors
　　　Yü and Yao!
Women clap their hands and sing, old men rise to dance—
Seedlings are planted, the rains are over, the sun sets in the west.

## COUNTRY SCENES IN LATE SPRING

KISEI REIGEN, *GBSS* II:200

1

In village after village there is joy, the shrines fragrant with wine,
With the 'grain rains' just clearing, farm work is busy;
Along sandy paths shadows weave drunkenly home,
As the sun goes down under the blossoms of paulownia trees.

2

Time to transplant rice-shoots now that the rains have ended;
An old fellow by a hedge in the flooded paddy fields,
Eyes filled with sons and grandsons—a real treasure!—
Has two, three cups of wine to celebrate the abundant harvest.

3

Straw raincloaks move along rice-paddies, now half mud,
Spring shoots maturing with the help of hoe and plow;
Cows and sheep know the road home at close of day:
The house to the west of where the cuckoo sings.

> *Poem dated 1439. The "grain rains," one of the 24 markers of
> the lunar agricultural calendar, last from 4/20 to 5/4. The
> cuckoo is known in China for his song* pu-ju-kuei, *"best to go
> home."*

## POEM WHILE LIVING AT DAIYŪJI TEMPLE (1)

NANKŌ SŌGAN, *GBSS* VI:261

I head for the market with three *sen* to buy pears and stroll about,
Chomping into the reddest, crunchier than plums;
This year, thank god, they're not "worth a thousand in gold"—
I can even afford one for the guardian deity Makora.

> *The last line of this poem contains the name* mogoraka, *from the Sanskrit* mahoraga, *originally a being with a human body and a snake's head. The word is used in Japanese to represent* makora, *one of the twelve fierce guardian deities.*

## CLOUDY WINE

KŌZEI RYŪHA, *GBSS* VII:182

New hay on the third of the third month, already getting sweeter,
Snow's behind us now in this river village and the prices are delightful;
Remember when I had to take my straw hat and robe to the pawnshop?
Now from the ridges of the thatched huts pokes a green tavern flag!

## SITTING ALONE IN THE MOONLIGHT:
## SENT TO SOMEONE WATCHING THE LANTERNS

GAKUIN EKATSU, *GBZS* III:2664 [706]

Lanterns in the city move to and fro, the moon bright as day,
Masses of busy people crisscross the city streets;
From the distance sounds of flutes and song float to the still temple
    among the pines
Where I keep the quiet of my mind through the long night.

> *The Lantern Festival was celebrated in China from the thirteenth to the seventeenth of the first month.*

RHYMING WITH A POEM: "PEOPLE'S DAY"

GIDŌ SHŪSHIN, *GBZS* II:1489 [613]

This ancient sight may add to people's days,
But each remaining year subtracts some teeth;
Palace-style coiffure is no concern of bald Zen monks—
Someone else will have to wear colorful hair ornaments.
Nowadays they use the Japanese *tachibana* instead of "Mandarin
    orange,"
The traditional bitter herb means nothing any more, has been turned
    to tea;
I need a metaphor for this lingering cold:
How about a shrivelled passion-flower?

> *The Chinese festival Jen-jih is humorously explored in its
> Japanese garb. Some of the attributes of this festival which
> occurred on the seventh day of the first month were colorful
> make-up and hair-ornaments for women, the orange (changed
> from the character read in Japanese as karatachi, "Chinese
> orange," to the more familiar native tachibana); and the tradi-
> tional herbal infusion made with a Chinese plant (whose archaic
> character has been turned into the more familiar "tea"). The last
> couplet contains a difficult pun: the flower is actually a "Flower of
> Tu-ling," long a Chinese expression for "singing girl." The En-
> glish translation must serve to render an untranslatable pun.*

NEW YEAR'S EVE, 1373, AND NEW YEAR'S MORNING, 1374:
TO SHOW TO MY DISCIPLES

GIDŌ SHŪSHIN, *GBZS* II:1406 [530]

1

I'm ashamed of myself, stealing these meals for three years,
But tonight's the end of the year and I can't stand it any more:
So, plum blossoms and bamboos by moonlight being my usual fare,
I've asked you in to treat you all to some.

2

On New Year's Day, people wish each other the longevity of the ancient
    Chinese Emperors,
Ladling out one gourdful after another of spring-rich 'long-life' saké;
I laugh to myself: how hard it is for monks to avoid these mundane
    customs—
In an unglazed bowl I steep tea to toast the New Year dawn.

## ON THE EIGHTH OF THE NINTH MONTH, 1349, THERE WAS A LIGHT SNOWFALL, WHICH I RECORDED IN A POEM

CHŪGAN ENGETSU, *GBZS* II:888; *GBSS* IV:350 [12]

In the ninth month at Rikonji snow's already in the sky,
Enormous trees ten armspans round have frozen and have to be cut
   down;
There never was flowering dogwood in Japan,
But even the yellow chrysanthemums have withered early because of the
   odd temperature . . .
And tomorrow is the Double Ninth! But with only cups of tea,
I don't see how we can properly celebrate the festival.
I've eaten all the red-bean rice and yellow leeks I can,
But the village children just make fun of me as a country priest with
   pretensions;
For an old fellow like me, it's no easy matter to "climb a high place"
When even the slippery mud outside my gate trips me up.

> The Chinese festival of the Double Ninth (that is, the ninth day
> of the ninth month) was also celebrated in Japan by Gozan
> monks. The poet laments the early snowfall, which has killed off
> the yellow chrysanthemums required for the traditional chry-
> santhemum wine, so that he will be forced to drink tea instead.
> The flowering dogwood, another Chinese symbol of the festival,
> does not grow in Japan as a native plant, as Chūgan says; it was
> first brought to Japan from Korea in 1720 as a medicinal herb,
> and is found in poetry only in the Chinese kanshi, not in the
> native waka.
> The "red-bean rice" and "yellow leeks" are also traditional
> foods associated with the festival in China, and from earliest
> times in China, people were expected to "climb to a high place"
> on this day in order to look out over a panorama and write
> poems suitable to the occasion. See A. R. Davis, "The Festival of
> the Double Ninth in Chinese Poetry," Chow Tse-tsung, ed.,
> Wen-lin (Ann Arbor: Univ. of Michigan Press, 1965), 49ff.

## END OF ANOTHER YEAR

MUGAN SOŌ, *GBZS* I:806

Time hurries along like an impatient colt,
A snake slithering down its hole, the tail of this year almost gone.
Is poverty going to leave with the old year?
For certain age will arrive with the new spring.
The affairs of this world make me hold my nose:
The stench of plum-blossoms has come round long enough.
It won't be *my* strength that props up the sect—
When my yam's done, just scatter the ashes in the hearth.

> *The Year of the Horse follows the Year of the Snake. For "yams," see p. 58.*

## PUPPETS

RYŪSEN REISAI, *GBZS* I:580

They function without feelings, yet gracefully,
Cavorting imperturbably, moved by divine inspiration;
Just add a line here—a Bodhisattva's face.
Take away some thread there—a Yaksha's head.

## 6. In China

China was the source of Buddhism for the medieval Japanese, the "homeland" of a religion whose Indian origins were by the twelfth century alien even to the Chinese. Chinese monks came to Japan as teachers, and the Japanese in turn made the "southern journey," as they called the trip to China, in search of teachers, texts and the famous sites of their sect's temples. The names of particular Chinese monks spread among the Japanese as those who welcomed visitors not always comfortable with the language, and the Japanese made the perilous voyage and trudged hundreds and thousands of miles to study with them. The Zen monks especially, much like the doctors of the medieval European universities, made the rounds of the leading figures of the day in order to test their mettle and gain recognition at home. They stood in line to have accommodating Chinese scholars write prefaces to their poetry collections so that they could boast to their friends back home. The Chinese, for their part, were less impressed with the Japanese monks' poems than with their willingness to pay large sums of money for these autographs.

One constant theme of the Japanese monk in China is, as we might expect, homesickness. The perils of travel, which included encounters with bandits and pirates and gouging petty officials, combined with the strange tongue that few Japanese could speak fluently and an intensely Japanese desire to be among their own, to leave even the hardiest Zen monk weeping alone in the small hours of the night.

If China was always alien to the Japanese, it also often did not live up to their expectations as the homeland of their religion. After the fall of the Southern Sung dynasty in 1279 to northern invaders—who had significantly failed to conquer Japan—the Japanese wrote more often of the vanished glories of what had been China than of the splendors before their eyes. To be sure, they were only borrowing the ancient Chinese poetic mode of *huai-ku*, "recalling the past with nostalgia"; but their poems of ruined temples and devastated sites are none the less ironic and touching for that.

In ruins or in its glory, for all that it may have been the homeland, China often seemed lacking in something to these monks, used to what was becoming over the centuries an entirely Japanese religion, even in its Chinese trappings. Japanese were starting to return home, from the beginning of the fourteenth century, to declare that they could not find Zen masters in China the equal of their own in Japan. One Japanese monk, a disciple of the great Kokan Shiren (who never went to China himself) came back grumbling sourly about "squandering Japanese gold for Chinese gravel."

---

## STAYING IN PAO-NING, 1325

CHŪGAN ENGETSU, *GBZS* II:898 [22]; *GBSS* IV:326

Not even a full year since I left my home temple,
Yet with what keenness I long to return to Japan!
My robe may have changed its colors,
But my Chinese still sounds as bad as it did before;
My clumsy poems produce ridicule—wearily I lay down my brush,
Wipe sweat from my sunken face, stifle my wretchedness.
The monks I traveled here with have scattered in all directions—
How frustrating to have no harmony for my brief song!

> *The date in the title should be 1326, the year that Chūgan actually reached Pao-ning in modern Szechuan Province. His discomfort with the Chinese language must have been especially galling in light of his avowed motive in going to China: "to get the Way and return to Japan to convert the masses."*

## RHYMING WITH AN IMPROMPTU POEM

BETSUGEN ENSHI, *GBZS* I:747

Beneath a flimsy thatched roof, I live in this strange land,
Heart ashen, ambition withered like a cut vine.
My homeland? I've given up trying to predict my return—
Heaven and earth will keep me waiting till I'm an old man.
Ten lonely years I've traveled over China,
And only in dreams can I return to my own hills and streams.
The lamp gutters, oil half gone; rain falls on the steps
As I try to recall a life that's already fading away.

## STAYING AT LU-YÜAN TEMPLE:
## WANG WEI'S FORMER RESIDENCE

SESSON YŪBAI, *GBZS* I:556; *GBSS* III:894

Dilapidated and deserted, this T'ang Dynasty temple,
The man who once lived here long since gone;
Over mountains folded like a thousand layers of silk,
A few sunset rays still linger in a transitory world.
Pagodas loom up out of mountain mists,
Bell sounds choke in the blowing wind . . .
Gazing from my window I put a halt to such regrets:
At the graveyard gate I'll meet him coming back.

> *Wang Wei (701–761) was a famous T'ang dynasty poet and Buddhist layman whose poetry was influenced by Buddhist thought. (See Introduction, p. 5.)*

## WHEN I PAID A VISIT TO OUR NEIGHBOR TO THE SOUTH

KEIJO SHŪRIN, *GBZS* IV:318

Poets of the T'ang, Sung, Yüan and Ming, and now we here in Japan,
Have all gone chasing after the Chinese wind and moon with our brushes,
When tangerines green all year round in the shrines of Otokoyama,
And plums redden for a thousand miles around the shrines of Dazaifu.
Among profuse, unopened reeds, like a chicken brooding an egg,
Or a cocoon of spun silk thread, the sun lies on the horizon:
With heavenly warp and earthly weft in lines of five and seven,
The gods help us to weave our poems of yellow silk.

> *The poet is saying that with the rich native Japanese traditions in art and poetry, there is no need to keep rushing to imitate the Chinese. He seems to deliberately contrast the green and red of Shinto shrines with the drab monotone of Zen temples. "Lines of five and seven" refer to the metrics of Japanese* waka *poetry, written in lines of 5-7-5-7-7 syllables.*

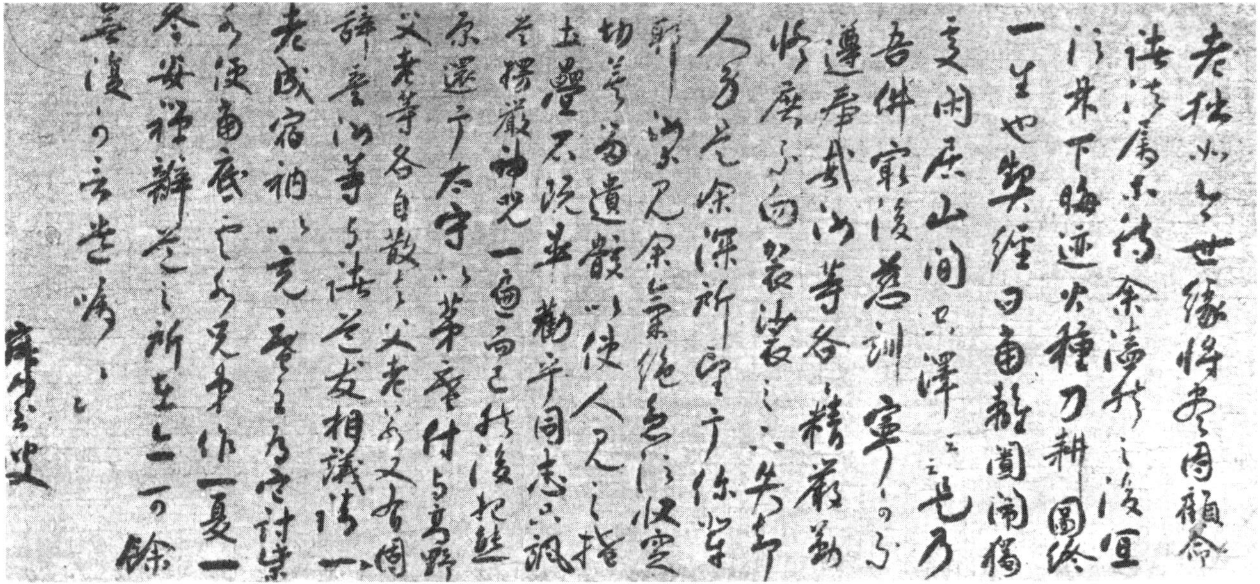

Calligraphy by Jakushitsu Genkō

## 7. Provincial Zen

I have pointed out in Chapter 4, "Living in Hermitage," that the medieval Japanese Zen monks were usually sent out or went on their own accord to small temples in the provinces to practice, seek solitude, deepen their enlightenment, and, no less important perhaps, to eke out a living. After all, only so many offices could be filled in the large metropolitan Gozan temples, and except for the monk who truly enjoyed the life of rural isolation, the competition for these positions was intense.

The result seems to have been a rural countryside populated with Zen monks of varying degrees of discontent. In small communities, where the people were invariably believers in the salvationary Amidist sects, the cold comfort of a resident Zen monk must have seemed altogether unsatisfactory. Nor was he any more enthusiastic at having to officiate at folk observances in which meat, wine, and trance-like calling upon the name of Amida Buddha figured prominently. Zen monks, usually by temperament as well as by training, were not likely to feel at home in a rural parish of poor farmers. We should recall that even in China, Ch'an Buddhism had always been attractive to and patronized by the upper-class literati, not the lower class believer in need of pious assurances of salvation. Many of the Gozan monks' poems tell of their unhappiness at being bothered by their rural neighbors, or by young zealots who invariably searched out the most recalcitrant and misanthropic hermits for instruction.

---

MOUNTAIN MARKET IN CLEARING MIST

KEIJO SHŪRIN, *GBZS* IV:183

The road passes through some mountain houses where the sun rises late
Amid soft greens, mist floating across the bridge . . .
It's not just idle talk that there are tigers in these villages,
People with human faces and animal hearts clawing for profit!

POEM IN REPLY TO A PARISHIONER

RYŪSEN REISAI, *GBZS* I:628

. . . And then you say you want a tombstone inscription for your
    son-in-law . . . ?
Excuse me, I should never have become involved in this discussion.
I'm out of wisdom—no more thoughts on the subject at all—
Shouldn't even have gone outside today.

THE LEAPING INVOCATION OF THE BUDDHA'S NAME (*ODORI
NEMBUTSU*)

NANKŌ SŌGAN, *GBSS* VI:215

On the fifteenth of the seventh month, the Festival of O-bon!
The children of Izumi and Settsu are in an uproar,
In the shrines lanterns hang from every beam,
Casting daytime colors along the shore.
The Chief of the Parade has selected the actors,
Red wigs cover the heads of those who beat the village drums:
They suddenly leap up, arms flailing, hands never at rest,
As mile after mile booms with empyrean thunderclaps.
Men dress in women's clothes, women imitate men,
In red kerchiefs, white caps, torn and tattered shirts,
Their mouths swell with cries of "*Namu Amida Butsu!*"
Till their *butsu-butsu-butsu* sounds like a pot bubbling over.
Heads bobbing, arms weaving, they crouch and straighten,
Divide and regroup again, tumbling crazily;
One gets laughs by imitating the hunchbacked priest—
They'll do anything, nothing is beyond them.
Then when energy's at fever pitch they begin the leaping,
And even the appointed officials go beserk.
As the Milky Way falls and the Dipper lingers in the north,
The bystanders form a paling standing in a circle;
And soon the dragons of the sea begin to dance as well—
On the autumn tide, the "lizard growls": rain's about to fall,
But on goes the *nembutsu* with a whoop and a row
As the simple folk in nine houses out of ten chime in.
The old spirits may return from year to year—
But with all this wretched wailing after the Buddha, *he* certainly won't
    come!

## PRAYING FOR AN ABUNDANT HARVEST, 1360

MUGAN SOŌ, *GBZS* I:798

The peasant folk have gathered to pray for a good harvest,
Rough saké-casks line up before the temple;
Still observing the ways handed down from olden times,
They've set up rushes to screen me from the sight of meat.
All kinds of mountain herbs, boiled and piled high:
Local mallows heaped on platters,
Mustard greens that make you sneeze,
Leeks pulled up from along the old riverbank,
Bean-curd in the Chinese style;
Provisions enough for an army, these turnip roots,
Rice white as the clouds on the mountaintops,
Dumplings round as the moon over the hills.
Seats have been provided in no particular order:
A hundred suffice for the entire village;
Assorted broths are passed around and slurped
With etiquette enough to fill a tome:
Several rounds in dried willow-knots,
Or dripping from old earthenware pitchers.
The drunker they get, the louder grows the din,
The autumn hills ashrill with cicadas.
Some like rainbow-serpents drinking up islands,
Others like whales sucking up rivers,
Bleary-eyed, they stare glassily upon the pillars,
Sprawl with legs outstretched, gawking at the roofbeams.
As the sport grows wild their yells turn inarticulate,
Sounds bubble up over and again as they enjoy themselves to the hilt—
Even women and children are treated to too much,
Each and every hand encircling a cup.
A beggar, clothes in a hundred patches,
Stick over his shoulder, leads his trained monkey—
But no one casts so much as a glance toward the hungry priest
Who swallows incessantly, mouth running with saliva.
Actors who have but a few poses,
Flute-players who can only screech:
Little talent, but they are treated generously—
Luckily, the rustic mob is in a good mood.

Their neighbor to the east is a lonely Buddhist
Who counts on their stupidity when he prepares his sermons;
Now, sweating, he watches from off to one side,
Embarrassed, uneasy and on his best behavior.
Millet and barley easily fluctuate in price,
An abundant harvest difficult to achieve,
So even though what he spews may not be golden,
Perhaps it's had some effect on the local gods . . .

Life isn't what it was in the old days—
Things have lost the roots they sprang from,
And anyone in a place where his accent is strange
Is looked on as fair game for duplicity.
In recent times armed soldiers have risen—
One ruler has fled to a Southern Court,
Another sits on the Imperial throne
With sharp spears at his back, swords behind the curtains.
All the valorous generals are short on strategy—
Whenever one looks up one sees predatory hawks.
The Emperor's rice-taxes fill the rebels' granaries,
While warriors piss on scholars' caps. . . .

The Great Man must settle matters
Or whose house will be safe to live in?
An empty nation, without a sovereign—
Through the harvest ripen, who will there be to eat it?
If they are so fond of the teachings of those ancient Wise Emperors,
They might also take some solace from the lessons of their history books;
But all they really esteem is their leather purses' bellies,
And have no stomach for "loyalty" or "right action."
The cloth in the royal robes is ageing,
The Emperor's spirit is enshrined as a cuckoo.
Every leaf on the tall pagoda-trees
With frozen sinews watches the frosty cold;
There are enough wronged birds to fill an ocean,
While foolish old men like me have moved off to the mountains,
Saying they haven't the strength to serve—
But who would reject even the slightest token of sincerity?

Men of great deeds, alas, are hard to find—
Why should I let such mundane matters vex me?
I laugh at that fellow stealing a swig,
Drunk and stuffed as a graveyard beggar after the funeral banquet;
The rest are also on their usual behavior,
Calmly ignorant of their own transgressions—
But it is not just they alone
Whose smiles shame turns to tears.

*Calligraphy by Ryūshū Shūtaku.*

## 8. Nature

The greater part of medieval Zen poetry, both in the monks' own collections and in this volume, is devoted to observation of the natural world. While entirely in keeping with the Chinese mode of writing poems about natural scenes, this might seem a somewhat frivolous activity for a monk who is supposed to be getting on with the solitary and aggravating business of seeking enlightenment. These poems, however, written though they sometimes were for aesthetic gratification, are perhaps the real core of Gozan poetry, for they reveal to the trained eye the Zen state of mind of the poet in a way that drier records of religious deeds and sayings do not. It is for this reason that the poems of Zen monks both in China and Japan were included in their recorded deeds and sayings (Japanese *goroku*)—although, to be sure, at the very end.

One type of poem observing nature is the minute description of a tiny scene, the poet attempting to extract the essence of its reality by focusing upon the crux of a paradox—a petal dancing in a spider-web although there is no breeze, the nature of plum-blossom shadows frozen in an ink-stone—and especially the manifold contradictions, apparent in our usual deluded state of consciousness, that are heightened or disappear under the gaze of the Zen poet.

Many of the scenes set down here were meant as inscriptions on ink paintings or fans, a favorite genre during the fifteenth century. These inscriptions are startling in their ability to evoke the paintings they were written on, now for the most part lost to posterity.

---

## WOMEN LADLING BRINE ON THE BEACH

BANRI SHŪKYŪ, *GBSS* VI:699

Brine ladlers—ugly women, black as crows,
Scrabbling with both hands at the salt that fills the sand;
They couldn't understand their wretched karma:
Yonder, buried in lime-smoke, tiny hovels on the bay.

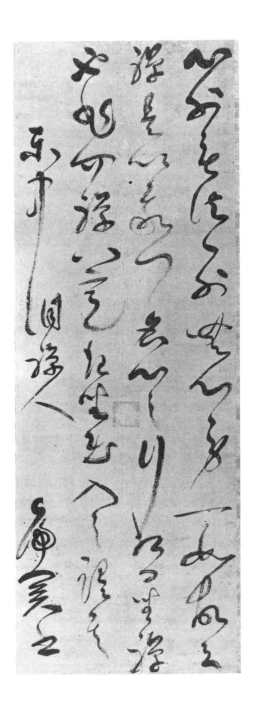

*Calligraphy by Kokan Shiren*

# EVENING RAIN IN A MAPLE FOREST

KEIJO SHŪRIN, *GBZS* IV:142


Evening clouds drag rain through remnants of maple leaves,
That fall, cold and eddying before the wind.
Just to amaze an old poet's eyes and ears
One gust turns the crimson wet; another, dry again.


# EVENING LIGHT ON CROWS' BACKS

KEIJO SHŪRIN, *GBSS* IV:297


Returning crows, like spattered ink beyond the skies,
The setting sun to their backs, shadows moving west,
Change in an instant as they join the evening clouds
To lines of poetry written by the wind on a black lacquer screen.


# SCROLL PAINTING

KEIJO SHŪRIN, *GBZS* IV:155


Everywhere, spring water burgeons in stream banks
Among the mountains of poetry in this painting:
White heads gleam: a pair of birds,
In this season when red faces slumber, drunk in the darkening green . . .


# ON A FAN

KEIJO SHŪRIN, *GBZS* IV:162


One edge of the sky ushers in the moon, another ushers out the sunset's
    glow,
Blurs of hazy light that join the bamboos' feathery green;
The brushwood gate by the old tree is still unlocked—
In the chill, crows all gone home, it waits for me to leave too.

## WINDOWS BROKEN, NO PAPER

KEIJO SHŪRIN, *GBZS* IV:115

I've meant to fix them but there's not a scrap of paper in my bag:
My windows are all broken—but there's no need to open them,
And the wind along the wall's edge snuffs out the lamp for me,
Rain from the eaves keeps my inkstone wet.

## SPRING ICE ON AN INKSTONE POND

KEIJO SHŪRIN, *GBZS* IV:106

The inkstone on my desk is locked in spring ice
In this late cold—the study door stays shut all day;
In the moon-toad water dropper I've stuck a sprig of plum-blossom:
Its shadow, frozen on the pond, can't drift away.

> *The small water container used for making ink in brush
> calligraphy was commonly made in the shape of the toad that
> legend says lives in the moon.*

## LINGERING SNOW AT THE VALLEY BRIDGE

KEIJO SHŪRIN, *GBZS* IV:81

The harsh wind and lingering cold don't know it's spring—
Where the valley's shade is deepest, snow remains in the early dawn;
Someone gathering firewood in the mountains
Has left footprints on the bridge at daybreak.

## ABOUT TO SNOW AT THE RIVER VILLAGE

KISEI REIGEN, *GBSS* II:220

Frozen clouds brewing snow wrap the river village,
In the wind rain-gear rattles its dry reeds,
While in the distance someone fishes on a bay already
Half turned to dusk by the fine sleet.

ON A FAN

KISEI REIGEN, *GBSS* II:241


The moon appears over the mountain-tops where swirling clouds open,
A crane flies to and fro on the other side of the river;
This mood, this moment—no place to set it down . . .
I wonder if the lad is coming along with that lute?


RED PEACH BLOSSOMS OVER THE WALL
OF A VILLAGE HOUSE

KISEI REIGEN, *GBSS* II:201


The path meanders in and out through villages and flooded fields:
Whose house could this be, its small peach tree so red?
Stray branches appear and disappear from behind the wall—
The gate to the bamboo grove is shut: must be guarding his blossoms.


EVENING CROWS

KISEI REIGEN, *GBSS* II:172


    1
Countless dots of crows flying home break up the evening sky,
Wings flapping, beak to tail over the far line of hills:
It reminds me of a place where children practicing calligraphy
Have spattered black ink all over the paper windows.

    2
So many crows flying home I can't tell east from west,
Hundreds and thousands flock together to fill the skies;
At the old temple on Cold Mountain under the maple leaves,
They clump together at the evening bell.

## ON A FAN: SPARROWS AND BAMBOO

KISEI REIGEN, *GBSS* II:172

A branch of bamboo stretched over the wall
Rises and falls unpredictably in the wind,
While sparrows, trying to perch for the evening, with unsettled hearts
Flutter up to it and then away again. . . .


## ON A FAN

KISEI REIGEN, *GBSS* II:192

Borne on gusts of wind from the river, the rain blows
Through countless green reeds that flower on the banks;
Straw cloak dancing on a leaf-like boat,
A fisherman, shouts growing fainter, heads into the billows.


## LANDSCAPE PAINTING WITH EGRET

KŌZEI RYŪHA, *GBSS* VII:333

Rivers and mountains linger in the red of the evening sun,
A white egret stays behind, its whole body autumn;
The sound of waves stirs in the trees along the sandy bank—
He would roost, but finds no branch to lodge on.

"Sparrows, trying to perch for the evening, with unsettled hearts
Flutter up to it and then away again"

*"A lone lad leads a small black ox"*

## INSCRIBED ON A FAN

KŌZEI RYŪHA, *GBSS* VII:195

In a scene of fragrant fields, willows wispy with haze,
A lone lad leads a small black ox,
Halter in hand, not a scheme in his head,
An embarrassment to a sleepy cloud of a white-haired Zen monk.

## COLD RIVER BANK: SMALL SCENE

KŌZEI RYŪHA, *GBSS* VII:180

Wild waves grow pale in the westering sun,
Egrets, calling to one another, head along the cold banks;
Where reeds and rushes, bent in half, conceal the high tide mark,
Purple crabs and yellow fish fill the evening mud.

## FISHING VILLAGE IN PALE SUNLIGHT

KŌZEI RYŪHA, *GBSS* VII:173

Windblown haze over the lake country still not settled by evening,
Late afternoon sunlight pale on the sand-bars;
Who would guess that someone's out here drinking,
Sun-bleached hair on dark waves in a boat come ten thousand miles?

## SHEPHERD'S FLUTE

ISHŌ TOKUGAN, *GBSS* II:862

Bamboo cut in the first full autumn moon
Blows with a metallic ring,
An ancient score the Pear Garden never knew,
A new music sprung from grassy bogs;
Beyond the crows the westering sun grows late,
The north wind springs up over the oxen
With a sound that rumbles in and shatters
Into sparrows chirping in country paddies.

> *The flute is said to have a "metallic ring" because autumn is traditionally associated with the "element" of Metal. The "Pear Garden" was the famous troupe of musicians and actors created by the T'ang Emperor Hsüan-tsung.*
>
> *Ishō may have been recalling a* waka *poem by Emperor Fushimi (1265–1317):*

| | |
|---|---|
| Hibikikuru | *The wind comes on,* |
| Matsu no ue yori | *Rumbling first among the pine trees,* |
| Fuchiokite | |
| Kusa ni koe yamu | *Blowing from their tops* |
| Yama no shitakaze | *And falling on the slopes below* |
| | *Till its voice grows silent in the grass.* |

*Gyokuyōshū* 15: 2172

## RIVER PLUM TREE IN THE TWELFTH MONTH

SEIIN SHUNSHŌ, *GBZS* III:2726 [768]

I don't like the plum trees at the Shogun's residence: red year after year,
They boast too much of wealth and beauty and drinking in spring
     breezes;
Better this single tree at the foot of a barren hill,
That opens before the year's end amidst the ice and snow.

## BAMBOO SHADOWS

SEIIN SHUNSHŌ, *GBZS* III:2712 [754]

Uneven bamboo shadows on still, dark moss,
Lie half across the front porch, half across the rear,
Some nearly gone, carried off by the setting sun,
While others approach with the rising moon.

## A PAINTING OF SOMEONE SLEEPING DRUNK ON A BOAT

SEIIN SHUNSHŌ, *GBZS* III:2705 [747]

Sunset: someone with wine aboard a stilled boat,
Green reeds at the estuary's mouth, white gulls;
His mind is not on the pleasures of fishing—
Out beyond the edge of the world, asleep, alone, drunk.

## DEW ON LOTUS PADS

GAKUIN EKATSU, *GBZS* III:2650 [692]

Autumn's crisp night air slips into the pond's banks,
Steadily building up dew on the unmoving lotus pads
So thickly that one fears that, grown round and heavy,
The green jade bowls will tilt and their crystal shatter.

## A SPRING WITHOUT BLOSSOMS

KEIJO SHŪRIN, *GBZS* IV:175

Peach and apricot trees in country village houses?
In this remote corner of Japan you'd think they didn't exist.
People's hearts are funny, always changing with circumstance:
In Kyoto, *anywhere* you go your eyes see blossoms!

## VIEWING BLOSSOMS AT KANNONJI AND EIMYŌJI

GIDŌ SHŪSHIN, *GBZS* II:1459 [583]

At Kannonji and north at Eimyōji,
Few visitors walk the secluded paths deep in spring;
On the single tree in an empty garden, blossoms like snow—
Incredible how few colors spring requires.

## TWO SCENES: INSCRIBED ON A SCREEN

GIDŌ SHŪSHIN, *GBZS* II:1437 [561]

1

Somewhere, a fishing boat arranges its lines—
Evening brings wind and rain, fishing's been slow;
From the houses on the shore on the other side of the willow trees,
A tavern flag gleams in a thicket of kitchen-smoke.

2

Evening snow hurries them homeward; the road twists, the going slow—
But why isn't the master riding on his donkey?
It walks alone, led by a country lad
To help it across the bridges over the gorges—no fear of danger.

> *In another poem, Gidō appears to have resolved the poignant
> separation in the first poem between the fisherman left on the
> lake at sunset and the inviting tavern in the distance:*
>
> *A tavern flag flutters, playing in the evening breeze,*
> *Inviting escape from heat in its green shade;*
> *Someone in a fishing skiff come seeking shelter*
> *Has pawned his rain-cloak to get drunk alone on board.*
>
> GBZS II:1470 [594]

## LANDSCAPE ON A FAN

GIDŌ SHŪSHIN, *GBZS* II:1349 [473]

Mist-bordered pine woods, a Buddhist temple,
At water's edge, willow trees, fishermen's huts;
Zen monk with empty bowl after noon,
Old fisherman drying nets in the setting sun.


## AT RIKONJI, WALKING IN THE SPRING: SIX-WORD-LINE POEMS

CHŪGAN ENGETSU, *GBZS* II:903 [27]; *GBSS* IV:338–39

1

Patches of snow here and there on the shaded banks,
Spring stream half flowing, half dried up,
Windy days, now cold, now warm,
Staff and sandals sometimes home, sometimes out.

2

Withered wisteria vines: twisting, writhing snakes,
Weird boulders: striped, crouching beasts;
Snow drifts and craggy chasms block the way,
Fluttering green spring returns to cover the scars.


## KAMADO-NO-SEKI: AFTER THE GENKŌ REBELLION, ON THE ROAD FROM HAKATA TO KYOTO

CHŪGAN ENGETSU, *GBZS* II:909 [33]; *GBSS* IV:328

The mountains of the Pass guard the harbor with a thousand walls,
Clouds of smoke from the houses blot out the evening sun;
"*Ee-aa*"—a scull-oar's creak breaks through the gloomy fog—
Startled into flight, a white egret passes over the dark waves.

## RHYMING WITH "EVENING VIEW ON THE RIVER": TWO POEMS

BETSUGEN ENSHI, *GBZS* I:743

### 1

The lone boat with its short oar skips along,
Men's voices hushed in the setting sun;
To the north and south of the river, willows line the banks,
And tavern flags flapping in the wind stretch out to the horizon.

### 2

As the azure glow declines, water and sky grow vaster,
On the river, an old fisherman angles alone in the cold;
Day turns to night but the boat with its pole still hasn't gone—
He's determined not to go back until he's caught a fish.

## MID-AUTUMN: BOAT MOORED AT CLEARWATER CREEK

SESSON YŪBAI, *GBZS* I:539

In a gorgeful of cold river encompassed by a ruler of sky,
The Milky Way hangs over the water, disturbs my sleep;
I prize the evening's moon for its extraordinary light—
No vermilion buildings with green doors here.

## EVENING LIGHT

RYŪSEN REISAI, *GBZS* I:617

The half disc of setting sun flattens into a corner of the mountains,
Its rays gleaming back up into the tree branches,
Spreading over the vault of the sky a lining of red shot silk
With a pale ink pattern of crows flying home to roost.

## BOAT IN THE MOONLIGHT

KOKAN SHIREN, *GBZS* I:92


Floating on the moon, my monk's boat winds through the reeds.
Tide's going out, the boy shouts, urging me back to the temple,
And village folk, thinking that a fishing boat's come in,
Scramble over the sand spit trying to buy fish from me.


## WINTER MOON

KOKAN SHIREN, *GBZS* I:93


Opening the window at midnight, the night air cold,
Garden and roof a gleaming white,
I go to the verandah, stretch out my hand to scoop up some snow—
Didn't I know that moonlight won't make a ball?


## IMPROMPTU POEM (9)

KOKAN SHIREN, *GBZS* I:105


The sky over the bay ahead a mass of cloud,
Now dark, now light, reflecting the setting sun's rays,
Back feathers light black, belly feathers white—
I watch the flock of sea birds turn and wheel in flight.


## EVENING STROLL

KOKAN SHIREN, *GBZS* I:121


Shadows of garden trees lengthen, wind sounds quicken,
As I slowly stroll through green sedge touched by setting sunlight;
Crows return together to reclaim the forest:
    The sun in their beaks
        The western hills
            Overflow with colored clouds.

## SPRING VIEW

KOKAN SHIREN, *GBZS* I:74

The world is renewed by the warm breeze and late sunshine;
Only I, in the face of this spring scenery, am ashamed of my old self.
Where does water leave off, sky begin? Both are azure blue,
Can't see trees for blossoms, everything reds and pinks;
Carts on outings and travelers' horses vie, racing along,
Swooping swallows and circling warblers frolic every which way.
Far-off villages, charming in their distant haze,
Locked in mist, willows along the road fade into the distance.

> *The expression "old self," uncommon in Chinese verse, appears*
> *in* waka *poetry, for example in* Kokinshū 28:

| | |
|---|---|
| Momochidori | *Although the spring* |
| Saezuru haru wa | *That brings the birds* |
| Monogoto ni | *Chirping in the trees* |
| Aratamaredomo | *Has renewed all things,* |
| Ware zo furiyuku. | *I alone remain my former self.* |

> *From the Buddhist, especially the Zen, point of view, the*
> *poet's "failure" to be reborn with the spring is ideal. The shift-*
> *ing of perspective and the uncertainty in the second couplet*
> *deny the unifying point of view of a "self." The effect is to blur*
> *the imagery further until it trails off into the false perspective*
> *of spring mists.*

## EVENING STROLL IN A SUMMER GARDEN

KOKAN SHIREN, *GBZS* I:95

My room so miserable with heat and mosquitoes I can't do zazen,
I kill time pacing the gravel paths, hands behind my back;
Nothing in the inner garden—something draws my attention—
Look closer: a single strand of spider web stretches across the path.

## IMPROMPTU POEM (29)

KOKAN SHIREN, *GBZS* I:106

From a spider's web hangs an empty cicada shell,
Twisting and turning this way and that in the breeze;
While it was alive one heard only its pleasant song—
Who would have thought that, dead, it could dance like this?

## WITHERED LOTUS PODS

KOKAN SHIREN, *GBZS* I:111

Lotus pods in late autumn touch my sympathies,
With broken sedge hats sprawled awry, twisted stems askew,
Seeds already gone—children plucked them all.
From an empty hole a wasp emerges, heading for his old nest.

## 9. Time and History

While this section includes some poems that were written while the poets were in China, there is something about them that emphasizes a universal sense of the passage of time and of history, rather than the particular quality of the experience of an alien land. Then, too, the medieval Zen monks also wrote poems about time and history in Japan. These poems are most often tragic in outlook, and transcend any one place and time as the poet looks out over a landscape whose dimensions are more properly moral than physical. The poems by Zekkai Chūshin and Chūgan Engetsu are especially moving, for these monks returned from the relative peace of China to a Japan in the throes of civil war. Poets wrote of the vanished glories of China, only to return home to find themselves writing of the vanished glories of Japan.

---

### IN IMITATION OF OLD

CHŪGAN ENGETSU, *GBZS* II:886 [10]

In the vast emptiness, in the winds of the end of an era,
Dust and dirt fly, whirling everything into confusion,
And in the sky the sun's color pales
As people, good and evil alike, struggle for ascendancy,
Maggots follow after putrid filth,
Rare birds betake themselves to haughty perches.
    Alone, a man who follows a way beyond these,
    Stands puzzled and distracted among the white clouds.

## OLD TEMPLE

ZEKKAI CHŪSHIN, *GBZS* II:1908 [1032]

Which way, deep in wisteria and ivy all around,
Does this ancient temple gate face?
Eaves have fallen like blossoms in the passing rains,
Wild birds caw right in one's face;
The image of the seated Buddha has sunk into the weeds,
The gold leaf of some wealthy donor peeled from its base;
No date remains on the fragment of stone inscription
To tell whether the temple dates from T'ang or Sung.


## THE STONE OF THE THREE WORLDS

ZEKKAI CHŪSHIN, *GBZS* II:1907 [1031]

Desolate, lonely T'ien-chu Temple,
A bit of stone resting among sharp peaks;
A thousand eternities have rubbed at it in vain,
A lingering dream of the Three Worlds, past, present and future.
At the roots of the clouds the mountain air is rich,
But grass fires have left patterns of dried moss;
Where are those two now, that met here once in another life?
Nothing but the wind, with its long, heartrending sighs.

> The collection T'ai-p'ing Kuang-chi *records the story of the*
> *"Stone of the Three Worlds," located at the T'ien-chu Temple*
> *at Hangchou in Chekiang province (where Zekkai studied with*
> *the Chinese master Chi-t'an Tsung-lao in 1372–73). The story*
> *tells of one Yüan Nan who came back to life to meet his friend*
> *Li Yüan there. Yüan had announced to Li that he would die,*
> *but would meet him at the rock twelve years later. Li returned*
> *on the date announced, and met an ox-herder who recited a*
> *poem that proved that he was, indeed, his friend Yüan. The tale*
> *illustrates the meeting of past, present, and future at a single*
> *point in time and space within the holy precincts of the temple.*

## CHIN-LING: IN REMEMBRANCE OF THE PAST

CHŪGAN ENGETSU, *GBZS* II:290 [24]; *GBSS* IV:326

The incessant friction of men's affairs has not worn down the earth one
    whit:
The Six Dynasties have vanished, but the mountains and rivers remain.
On the ancient ruins of gold-filigreed palaces sit merchants' and
    fishermen's houses,
Over the lingering sounds of jade trees waft the songs of woodcutters
    and shepherds;
Across rows of valleys cloud after cloud brings the usual rain,
The Yangtze River, the wind now settled, still raises its billows.
The handsome men and women of those days—where are they now?
A visitor from far over the seas is left with painful memories.

> *Chin-ling is another name for modern Nanking in Chiangsu
> Province. Successive cities on this site were mourned by later
> poets under the early name Chin-ling as a symbol of the van-
> ished splendors of the past.*

## AKAMAGASEKI

ZEKKAI CHŪSIN, *GBZS* II:1920 [1044]

The scene before me brings sorrow night and day:
A cold tide battering the red walls,
Among weird crags and fantastic boulders, a temple in the clouds,
Between the new moon and the setting sun, boats on the sea.
A hundred thousand valiant warriors have turned to empty silence,
Three thousand swordsmen are gone forever;
Heroes' bones rot in a soil of shields and lances—
Thinking of them, I lean on the balustrade, watch the white gulls.

> *This poem alludes to a famous battle in the civil war between
> the Taira and the Minamoto clans at Dannoura in 1185.
> Akamagaseki lies outside the modern city of Shimonoseki at the
> southernmost tip of Honshu. See also commentary on Chūgan
> Engetsu's poem "Dannoura" that follows.*

## DANNOURA: AFTER THE GENKŌ REBELLION, ON THE ROAD FROM HAKATA TO KYOTO

CHŪGAN ENGETSU, *GBZS* II:909 [33]; *GBSS* IV:327

Mist lies across the evening bay, shot through with rays of setting sun
Sent off sadly by fishermen's songs, falling on white shore-flowers;
How many great warriors died here?
The bones of their wars are dried, bleached piles of white sand.

> *Dannoura, at the strait of the west end of the Inland Sea
> between Honshu and Kyushu in what is now the city of Shi-
> monoseki, was the site of one of the most famous of the battles
> between the Taira and Minamoto clans in the wars that brought
> the Heian period to an end in 1185. Chūgan's reference to the
> site is meant to allude to the political confusion of his own time
> during the attempt by Emperor Go-Daigo in 1333, during the
> Genkō Rebellion, to wrest political power away from the Hōjō
> regents. At this time, Chūgan had only just returned to Japan
> from China.*

## REGRETTING TIME'S PASSAGE: IMPROMPTU POEMS

CHŪGAN ENGETSU, *GBSS* IV:352

1

Many years ago today Kamakura fell,
The temples that remained have all changed with the times;
But the merchant women can't know how much a monk regrets
Their selling firewood and vegetables right in the temple roads.

2

Affairs of the world rise and fall, each in their time,
The mountains and rivers remain—only the people don't;
Where the bones of war still lie uncollected, frontier guards spring up,
And Zen robes gradually become those of Confucians.

> *The second line of the second poem echoes a famous line of the
> poem "Spring View" by the great T'ang poet Tu Fu: "The
> country in ruins, only mountains and rivers remain."*

RHYMING WITH THE POEM "PASSING THE MINAMOTO
GENERAL'S FORMER KITAYAMA RESIDENCE"

ISHŌ TOKUGAN, *GBSS* II:890, 991

Spring arrives at the mansion's pond as if it hadn't come at all:
Zen monks, their mouths sealed, sit still as rocks,
While swallows in pairs twitter their regrets in the front hall
Of days when the jewelled blinds and filigreed doors were open. . . .

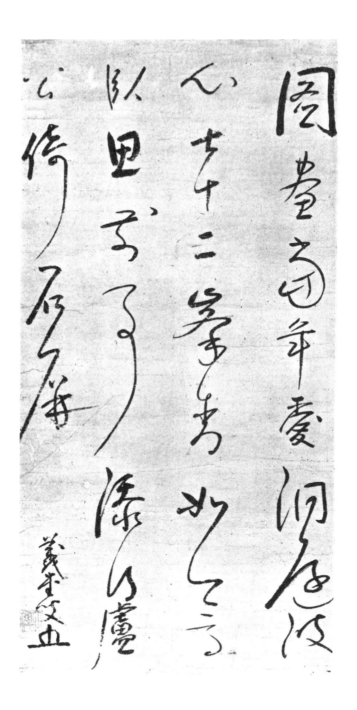

*Calligraphy by Gidō Shūshin*

## 10. Fame, Fortune, and Old Age

The Gozan monks wrote often of private regrets, even while realizing that as Zen monks they were not supposed to be prey to regret, or for that matter any other uncontrollable emotion. And yet, age crept up on them and hair whitened—a Chinese conceit that seems out of place among shaven-headed monks—and the fact that they had never attained high office, or that they *had* attained high office and had little time for anything else, became problems that continued to vex them. The tragedy of old age, as a French author once wrote, is that we do not *feel* old. It should be remembered that these monks followed the Chinese in picturing themselves as old men even when they were twenty-five; since Gozan monks regularly lived to be more than seventy, they presumably had a great deal of time to perfect the poetic treatment of regret for the passing years.

---

### CROWS AT EVENING IN A MAPLE FOREST

KEIJO SHŪRIN, *GBZS* IV:82

The mountain path climbs and climbs in the chill sunset
Through a forest full of maple leaves like crows about to take flight;
Young folks don't understand the way an old man thinks—
To these drunken eyes, they're blurred blossoms of falling ink. . . .

### ON "DRAWING ONE'S SWORD TO DRIVE OFF OLD AGE"

KISEI REIGEN, *GBSS* II:215

There's a saying about "drawing one's sword to drive off old age";
But when you're old, there's no strength left for such silliness,
And little profit to be had in fooling around with blades
When one's heroism has all gone the way of one's hair. . . .

## BLOSSOMS ARE NOT COMPANIONS OF OLD AGE

KISEI REIGEN, *GBSS* II:199

Don't sit there at your wine and laugh at my white head!
Youth could never understand an old man's melancholy:
We live to seventy—I'm past halfway there,
And death doesn't wait till we've seen the spring blossoms.


## THANKING SHINDEN FOR HIS VISIT

KŌZEI RYŪHA, *GBSS* VII:228

A rented house, recently completed, on the shady side of the lake:
How could this white head be any happier? I've put an end to dusty
    designs.
Talking over old times with a monk from the capital, the night already
    half over,
The lakeside temple grows colder, snow a foot deep all around;
Please don't recall those painful memories of the past. . . .
These mountains now—so lovely, how could I ever go back?
When you return, should my old temple friends ask of me,
Tell them I feel the past forty-seven years are as nothing. . . .

   *Shinden Seiha (1375–1447) was the poet's best friend.*


## POEM TO RHYME WITH DOMBU'S "POEMS AT JŌRAKUJI TEMPLE"

GIDŌ SHŪSHIN, *GBZS* II:1405 [529]

The frosty wind last night got into my unlined quilt
And brought back a whole lifetime's unceasing regrets:
If I'm too lazy to take a needle to my torn robe,
How am I to keep autumn out at four in the morning?

## THE MONK DAISEN OF ZENPUKUJI TEMPLE PAID ME A VISIT; I WROTE THIS POEM, USING HIS RHYMES, TO THANK HIM

MUSŌ SOSEKI, *TD* 80:477a

I thought with a hide as tough as mulberry bark I could live beyond the
 waves of the world,
But busy mouths that could melt iron followed me everywhere;
Just when I had muted my emotions to the hues of pale mist,
My sweet, dark dreams were shattered by the sound of the evening tide.
High in a cranny of the mountains one forgets their dangers,
And living near the ocean tells one little of its depths:
If I don't cut myself off completely at this pass,
Giant waves a thousand fathoms high will overwhelm my temple gate.

> *Daisen Dotsu (1264–1339) of Zenpukuji in Sagami was in the
> line of the important Chinese monk Ta-hsiu Cheng-nien
> (Daikyū Seinen, 1215–1289). Musō refers in the poem to a peri-
> od of very real danger to his career following his resignation as
> abbot of Nanzenji in 1326—a position delicately balanced
> between two feuding Imperial factions—and his return to the
> Kamakura area. The expression "important pass" (literally
> "important river-crossing") echoes the last words of a lecture in
> the works of his teacher Kōhō Kennichi in which he speaks of
> giving up "dreams" of high position in the temple world.*
>
> *It is interesting to compare this poem in Chinese to a* waka
> *poem by Musō entitled "Yokosuka on the Miura Penninsula in
> Sagami is a jagged coastline of sea and land; for some time
> (1320–23) I lived there in a hermitage I built":*

| | |
|---|---|
| Hikishio no | *There is a sound* |
| Ura tōzakaru | *As the tide draws far out* |
| Oto wa shite | *Into the bay,* |
| Higata mo miezu | *But I cannot see the tidal flats—* |
| Tatsugasumi kana. | *The mist has risen.* |

*GSRJ* IV:360B; *ST* V:161:2

## HIMSELF

KOKAN SHIREN, *GBZS* I:73

Crooked Zen chair, motley Zen robes—
Stolen the name of a Zen monk without any Zen to me,
My bookish ways and lack of direction
Have earned me some evil names:
"Zen Master *Treatise on the Heart of the Buddha's Words,*"
"Compiler of the *History of the Monks.*"

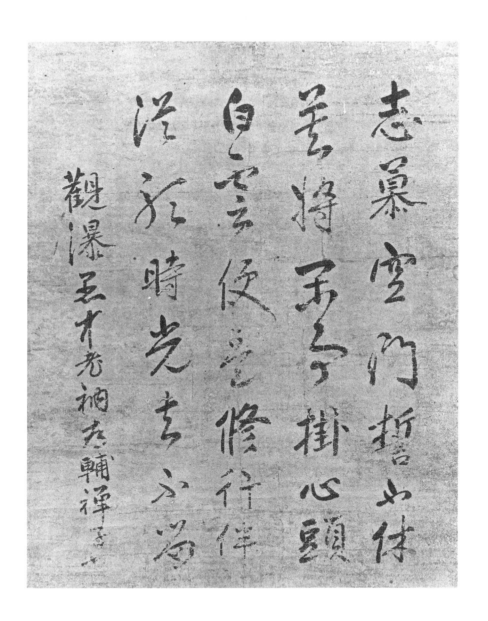

*Calligraphy by Guchū Shūkyū*

## 11. Weather and the Changing Seasons

The weather and changing seasons were an unfailing source of inspiration for Zen poetry. What better illustration of the principle of "permanence in mutability" could there be, after all, than the constant rotation of the seasons? What better illustration of impermanence than unseasonal weather that brought blossoms in the dead of winter, snow in late spring, freezing rain in summer, scorching heat in autumn? Then too, there was the paradox of the reality of the Japanese weather in each season in its encounters with the alien Chinese calendrical markers of the agricultural year. I have left poems about cherry blossoms and maple leaves to the section on nature, including here only those poems that explore the contradictions of the seasons in Zen terms.

---

### SWEEPING LEAVES AND POURING PINE WINE

KEIJO SHŪRIN, *GBZS* IV:271

Face redder than maple leaves at sunset, a monk
Pours himself pine wine into a cup of knobby wisteria;
Once drunk by the hearth, spring fills the room—
And I don't even have to go out into the night to chop ice for tea.

### SPRING, THE CITY OF THE COLOR OF RAIN

KEIJO SHŪRIN, *GBZS* IV:181

Spring in the city can't compare with the dry sunlight of autumn:
The morning colors blur together as rain obscures the crabapple trees,
The air makes everything seem as though seen through unfocused eyes,
A dusty haze through which, dimly, appears someone out looking for
    blossoms.

## WRITING A SPELL TO PROTECT BLOSSOMS

KEIJO SHŪRIN, *GBZS* IV:133

Wind and rain just as the blossoms are falling!
I laugh as I write an incantation to hang on the flowering branches;
People returning home sobering up from their wine will have a hard
     time reading *this*—
Slanting across the sparse plum shadows, a poetic charm in Sanskrit.


## A MESSAGE TO SOMEONE WHOSE BLOSSOMS
## I SAW FROM A DISTANCE

KISEI REIGEN, *GBSS* II:219

Far off there in the distance—is that a peach tree? an apricot?
Up to the gate without bothering to ask whose house it might be;
The whole spring, just like some crazy butterfly,
I'll go anywhere for the sake of blossoms.


## CLOUDY IN SPRING—ABOUT TO SNOW

KŌZEI RYŪHA, *GBSS* VII:212

The season for picking tea, and still I'm afraid to go out in unlined
     robes,
As clouds brew up a fresh cold, snow's about to fly;
Having sung those poems about how hazy tonight's spring moon will be,
I stand and wait now for a hail storm through the fresh green of the
     willows.

## PAINTING OF AUTUMN TREES AT THE EVENING BELL

ISHŌ TOKUGAN, *GBSS* II:857

Eastern and western foothills
Gaze across at one another under lowering skies.
A faint bell hurries the setting sun,
A few strokes falling in the wind;
Leaves stripped from trees, nowhere to go,
Their mist has already deserted the willows:
Winter's approach
    Makes the ancient temple
        Even more desolate.

## HEARING THE SOUND OF CLOTH BEING FULLED

ISHŌ TOKUGAN, *GBSS* II:855

The soldiers are still not recalled from the suburbs,
Yet already the first of the autum fulling is heard;
Lengthening nights intensify passions in the inner chambers,
And the first cold, homesickness in the frontier camps.
By a lone lamp, the shadow of an overturned pestle,
A shattered mirror, a snapped sword-hilt. . . .
I rise, startled by the geese in the skies,
One sound ceaselessly following another.

## FAN LANDSCAPES

GIDŌ SHŪSHIN, *GBZS* II:1423–24 [547–48]

    1
Autumn brings its cruel heat, humid as ever.
Not home to visitors, I stretch out to sleep, too dull to greet anyone;
Suddenly a fresh breeze blows me from my dreams—
Over the river rises a few peaks' green.

    2
It looks like south China, this hamlet, set amid water and bamboo.
A sail lowers: someone's recognized his brushwood gate;
In the sunlit tops of maple trees on the opposite bank,
Roost a few dots of crows scattered like ink from a drunken painter's
    brush.

## INSCRIBED ON A FAN

MUGAN SOŌ, *GBZS* I:800

Last year when the cool breezes arose,
I folded you back in your case;
Now once again the heat is upon us,
And again I've got you by the handle.
Coming out and hiding away—everything happens according to heaven,
Yet you betray neither anger in one nor joy in the other,
But with the gracious, generous spirit of a great man,
Deign to mingle with us frivolous and fickle sorts.


## ON THE NINETEENTH I ARRIVE AT CHUNGKING: SUFFERING FROM HEAT ON BOARD

SESSON YŪBAI, *GBZS* I:540, *GBSS* III:877

First Chia-chou in the seventh month, depressed by enervating rains;
Now Yü-chou in the eighth, plagued by late summer heat.
Mountains and rivers everywhere in this alien world,
And nature that toys with men who hurry along this way.
What is there to say about such ill-behaved temperature?
On a river once dangerous with wind and wave,
Now, with drawn-out moans, poling the boat through tangled
    water-plants, we float on a canopy of jade,
Eyes brightening only as white birds cross the hazy bay.

## AUTUMN WHITE

SESSON YŪBAI, *GBZS* I:548; *GBSS* III:885

Autumn gusts circle a gleaming silver disc
Whose light falls on the clear river, a bolt of cold glossed silk;
Although the banks are strewn with red thistle flowers,
A Zen monk sees it all in monochrome.

> *This poem has been interpreted as an attack on the rigid
> traditional Chinese metaphysical scheme that equates the sea-
> son autumn with the color white, reading the word Tao-jen,
> "man of the Way," in the last line as "Taoist." Certainly this
> scheme is alluded to in the title and is necessary to an under-
> standing of the poem.*
>
> *One suspects, however, that the significance of the poem
> goes deeper than this. Sesson understands and plays on the
> traditional metaphysical equation with the Buddhist concept of
> "color" (shiki), the manifold but ultimately illusory differentia-
> tions that comprise what we think of as reality, reduced by
> bright moonlight in this as in so many of the Zen monks'
> poems, to its actual "colorless" (monochrome) reality.*

## BEGINNING OF AUTUMN—FIRST OF THE SEVENTH MONTH

SESSON YŪBAI, *GBZS* I:538; *GBSS* III:875

Infinitesimal in the eternal flux, all things are travelers,
And the haste with which months and years go by is alarming;
Leaves around the pagoda trees rustle an autumnal message,
Wind through the duckweed hurries off the heat as a parting gift;
The Min Mountains are cold with the color of snow,
But the sound of waves on the Min River has not yet stilled:
My boat ties up—somewhere a cicada's shrilling quickens.
Over the mountain temple, greenery darkens in the evening light.

> *This poem was written while Sesson was in Ch'eng-tu, the
> capital of the present province of Szechuan. The Min Moun-
> tains and Min River are major scenic attractions accessible from
> the city.*

## START OF SUMMER: AN IMPROMPTU POEM

MING-CHI CH'U-CHUN, *GBZS* III:2022

After the rain the tepid heat is still cut by a slight chill,
Though they say that in the outskirts to the south spring is finally over;
Warblers chirp on willow branches with a note still harsh,
Cicadas shrill in the pagoda trees but their sound is tentative;
In the mood to ply a palm-leaf fan, I leave it stored away,
Start to open the ivy-covered window, then close it again
And remember how it was this season last year—
Cool breeze on my face, enjoying the secluded stillness.

> *The "Start of Summer" is one of the twenty-four ancient
> Chinese calendrical terms that divided the agricultural year. It
> occurred in the fourth month of the old calendar, and is
> equivalent to the beginning of June now and the advent of the
> rainy season in Japan. Ming-chi may have been in China in
> "this season last year."*

## SPRING

KOKAN SHIREN, *GBZS* I:74

Gentle breezes and warm sunshine fill every mountain cranny,
But this temple garden is still dreary, sealed in green moss;
Blossoms, when I chance to see them, turn their smiles to me,
Warblers, unasked, bring me their songs;
Here where spring's poignancy is attenuated I blow a reed flute,
As dreams linger into noon, sip tea from a bowl.
Swallows, untroubled by the fine spring days,
Circle back and forth, carrying mud in their beaks.

## BEGINNING OF AUTUMN

KOKAN SHIREN, *GBZS* I:96

The heat's full intensity hasn't abated one whit,
So where does this sensation of coolness come from?
I take my time, concentrate, listen—there it is again:
Falling paulownia leaves and chirping crickets have joined in a new
      sound.

## AUTUMN NIGHT: SITTING ALONE

RYŪSEN REISAI, *GBZS* I:584

The dark clouds have cleared away again in meditation,
Now and then, a snatch of moonlight comes through cracks in the eaves;
In the night I listen to the forest wind brush and whip the branches:
Rustling, it flings the leaves down, touching bare branches into song.

## BEGINNING OF AUTUMN

RYŪSEN REISAI, *GBZS* I:605

The weather this morning is much as it was yesterday,
The dawn bell finds no fewer geese on the canal;
Yet, for no good reason, a single leaf comes fluttering down,
Just because people have decided that autumn starts today.

> *The conceit is common in waka poetry; compare for example a poem by Mibu no Tadamine, "Composed at a Poetry Contest at the House of Taira Sadabumi" (the English translation is that of Brower and Miner in* Japanese Court Poetry, *p. 183):*

| | |
|---|---|
| Haru tatsu to | *Is it just because* |
| Iu bakari ni ya | *They say this is the day which marks* |
| Mi-Yoshino no | *The coming of spring* |
| Yama mo kasumite | *That the mountains of fair Yoshino* |
| Kesa wa miru ran. | *Are veiled this morning in a haze?* |
| | *Shūishū,* I:1 |

> *According to the Chinese lunar calendar, the Beginning of Autumn falls on the fifth day of the eighth month.*

## 12. Travel, Outings, and Excursions

Travel was for Zen monks a fact of life as they moved from one temple to another, often in widely separated areas of Japan. Travel is one of the great themes of poetry in China as well. But for the Zen monk, it was seen as another opportunity to illustrate the Path that the seeker for enlightenment traveled, the stopping-points along which he regarded as only temporary dwellings in an impermanent world. In the words of the the old Zen adage, "To walk the Way is to put one foot after the other" (see poem on p. 25).

Outings and excursions into the countryside, however, were entirely another matter. The monks enjoyed the chance to take such trips, with their opportunities for drinking *saké* and writing happy poems about cherry blossoms. Their superiors might have disapproved, had they not been so busy going on outings with the noble and warrior aristocracy themselves.

---

### FISHING CASH

The *Jirin Kōki* says that coins strung together by a thong through the hole are called "fishing cash" [*tsurigane*]. Today I received ten strings from the bakufu office to pay for my trip home.

BANRI SHŪKYŪ, *GBSS* VI:755

The government has given me a year-end present of ten strings of
   "fishing cash"—
Even more wretched than last year's bone-piercing poverty!
In the kitchen, I sleep with the dismal howl of wind in the pines,
Haven't even got a pot to gather dust in. . . .

LEFT HIRASAWA'S INN AT TAKEKURA
FOR HACHIGATA TO THE NORTH

BANRI SHŪKYŪ, *GBSS* VI:741

Scrawny horse in deep mud, stumbling through hills and rivers—
Why doesn't a night's sleep cure these hangovers?
Thirty-six mornings now with nothing else to do
But chuckle at how many bad poems I've inscribed on fans.

ON THE ROAD TO RYŪMONJI ("DRAGON GATE TEMPLE")

BANRI SHŪKYŪ, *GBSS* VI:659

Heel and toe, heel and toe, mountain after mountain;
"Dragon Gate" must be up there in the evening clouds!
I knock at the door of a teashop to ask the way—
The evil-looking old crone's voice still rings in my ears.

FOR A BATH AT KAKEZUKA THEY CHARGED 100 PIECES

BANRI SHŪKYŪ, *GBSS* VI:697

Boat arrives at Kakezuka—out of my traveling clothes,
But 100 pieces of copper to get into the bath!
Seafood meal gritty with sand, food completely tasteless,
Wind strikes the nostrils with the reek of fishermen's huts. . . .

## SARCASTIC THANKS TO YŌSHIN FOR HIS GIFT OF PAPER FOR SERVICES RENDERED

BANRI SHŪKYŪ, *GBSS* VI:740

When I go on outings with friends, I always get a pint of wine or some fine calligraphy or poetry in exchange for writing out fair copies [of the day's poetry]. Never have I heard of getting a ream of rough mulberry paper, and yet for a total of 500 words I was given fifty sheets—a mere sheet for every ten words!

Paper so thin you'd have to fold sheet upon sheet to make a robe for a
    butterfly,
Persimmon leaves withered in the frost at Ssu-en temple:
The water in the inkstone on my desk is still dried up—
Hurry up with that gift pint of village wine!

> *The second line refers to the story of the Chinese monk Cheng-ch'ien, who practiced calligraphy at the Ssu-en Temple on persimmon leaves instead of paper; Banri is making fun of the poor quality of the rough paper.*

## INSCRIBED ON A PAINTING

KEIJO SHŪRIN, *GBZS* IV:201

The sun sinks into the western hills, the road winds ahead,
Several miles still to go before we see a house;
Servant's tired, donkey's faltering, inspiration's gone,
And fine sleet blurs the blossoms on the ancient trees.

## VIEWING BLOSSOMS AT A MOUNTAIN TEMPLE

KEIJO SHŪRIN, *GBZS* IV:84

The road enters green mountains near evening's dark;
Beneath the white cherry trees, a Buddhist temple
Whose priest doesn't know what regret for spring's passing means—
Each stroke of his bell startles more blossoms into falling.

> *Keijo surely had in mind a famous* waka *poem by the Heian priest Nōin (998–1050), "Composed When I went to a Mountain Village":*
>
> | Yamazato no | *As now I come* |
> |---|---|
> | Haru no yūgure | *And see the spring day grow to dusk* |
> | Kite mireba | *In the mountain hamlet,* |
> | Iriai no kane ni | *The cherry blossoms fall to earth* |
> | Hana zo chirikeru. | *At the sounding of a temple's vesper bell.* |
>
> *Shinkokinshū,* II:116; translated in Brower and Miner, *Japanese Court Poetry*, p. 185.

## TRIP TO A VILLAGE TEMPLE ON THE FIRST OF WINTER

KEIJO SHŪRIN, *GBZS* IV:82

Crows' backs—mountains darkening in the twilight sun,
Wind blows sere leaves through the ancient Zen temple;
In the village, early winter cold made all the colder
By the sound of a bell from a city temple down where there's still no
    frost.

## RHYMING WITH YOUNG MONK SETTEI'S POEM AT NEW YEARS

KISEI REIGEN, *GBSS* II:208

It's not as much fun to go traveling now as it was on a bamboo horse:
When you're old, you realize how hard it is to ride red-faced;
How pleasant it must be to know only the joy of welcoming the spring,
Not having to fret that the color of the blossoms is creeping into your
    hair.

*"The road enters green mountains near evening's dark"*

## BUYING VILLAGE BREW

KISEI REIGEN, *GBSS* II:214

Village brew isn't weak, always sour or sweet,
But the credit's easy and the price is right;
It fortifies me for poetry and my lame donkey for the snow—
In the thatched tavern by the country bridge, we watch the tavern flag
    flap in the wind. . . .


## BAMBOO HORSE

KISEI REIGEN, *GBSS* II:208

We cut bamboo stalks to make horses—what fun we had playing then!
And looked forward to the time we could harness up a team and drive a
    big carriage;
Now, late in life, I'm carrying out that childhood desire—
Freezing in the wind-driven snow for the sake of a poem, whipping a
    lame donkey. . . .


## COUNTRY BRIDGE: LINGERING RAIN

KŌZEI RYŪHA, *GBSS* VII:173

Shapes of trees loom faintly from the other shore,
Visible in the distance across the setting sun's rays, through sheets of rain
That wind sends circling the bridge and off toward the south,
Leaving behind a man on horseback, drenched and dismal.

## AUTUMN: EVENING OUTING TO A MOUNTAIN TEMPLE

SEIIN SHUNSHŌ, *GBZS* III:2752 [794]

I've chanced upon a temple high in the mountains
Where the autumn wind is full of the past:
Temples, too, have their creation and destruction,
Flourish and decay with the affairs of men;
On the antique green of moss untended in the rain,
The new red of leaves, fallen in the frost—
I press no further, but ask the way back
To the city, yellow with the dust of horses.

> *"Temple high in the mountains" can be read as Kozanji, the ancient temple atop Mt. Takao to the northwest of Kyoto.*

## HOT SPRING: IMPROMPTU POEM

TESSHŪ TOKUSAI, *GBZS* II:1302 [426]

### 1

Eyes filled with yellow dust, I arrived ill and weary,
A leaf fallen from a green tree that couldn't stand the autumn;
But having finished my hot soak, everything is fine again—
If it just weren't for these horse-flies lighting on my head. . . .

### 2

Bramble gate half shut, I still feel the cold chill
Of pale autumn sunshine on Mt. Rokko;
A lame monk leaning on a cane begs from door to door—
Too bad he came all this way without a store of provisions. . . .

*"Traveling, I come to a house in the mountains just at noon"*

## AN OUTING TO THE TŌGETSU BRIDGE TO LOOK
## AT BLOSSOMS IN ARASHIYAMA

CHŪGAN ENGETSU, *GBZS* II:914 [38]

1

Wild clouds toward evening bring the blossoms' fall closer—
I regret that by tomorrow morning the rain will have decimated them,
So to solace our old age, I've come outside the temple gates to visit—
People lean all along the bridge's railing, forget to go home.

2

Arashiyama's mists force the blossoms to fall, petal by petal,
The whole mountain patches of thinning white hair;
Halfway over the river the moon is pale, water like a mirror—
I see my ageing face in its reflection, ashamed at wanting to go home.

> *The Tōgetsu ("Crossing to the Moon") Bridge spans one end of
> Lake Arashiyama in the western outskirts of Kyoto. The view
> from one side of the bridge faces Mt. Arashiyama, a mass of
> cherry-blossoms in the spring and of maple leaves in the fall.*

## WALKING IN THE MOUNTAINS

MUGAN SOŌ, *GBZS* I:810

Tiring to the feet but refreshing to the eyes,
This wandering with a cane through mist and fog;
Hard to tell if it's real or a painting—
Against a pale wash of cold woods, the dark ink of crows.

## HOUSE IN THE MOUNTAINS

MING-CHI CH'U-CHUN, *GBZS* III:1993

Traveling, I come to a house in the mountains just at noon.
Folks in these parts aren't used to seeing travelers:
A dog yaps at me through a hole in the bamboo fence,
An old man, warming his back under sunny eaves, yawns and stretches.

## SEEN ON THE ROAD

MING-CHI CH'U-CHUN, *GBZS* III:1993

Broken bridge: on the other bank, a few houses,
A windblown flag stuck at an angle, a privet hedge,
And a stupified old gent lying sprawled asleep,
Unaware that his hair is white as the blossoms.

> *The "flag" in these poems is always the pennant that indicates a
> tavern. The "privet hedge" is the plant that may be translated
> as "Rose of Sharon," "Althea," or just "mallow," bearing white
> flowers that bloom and fade in a day and so, like white hair, a
> symbol of past glory.*

## 13. Friendship

Except for the few true hermits among them, the Gozan monks were a very social lot, and every time they invited, met, visited, consoled, commiserated with, congratulated, or parted from a friend, out came writing-brush and paper for the inevitable poem. These few poems illustrate some of the aspects of friendship in the Gozan.

---

### WILD CAMELIAS

GIDŌ SHŪSHIN, *GBZS* II:1389 [513]

This old temple is dreary, half obliterated by moss—
Who would ever park his carriage before *my* gate?
But the servant-boy, knowing I've asked someone over,
Has carefully failed to sweep the camelia-blossoms that strew the
    ground.

### COLD NIGHT: IMPROMPTU

JAKUSHITSU GENKŌ, *TD* 81:103a

Wind stirs the cold woods, a frosty moon gleams,
Absorbed in talk of elevated things, midnight come and gone,
(Roast yams on skewers lie forgotten in the hearth)
Silently we listen to the sound of leaves raining on the window.

## THE MONK HŌGAI OF SEIGENJI SENT ME A POEM;
## I USED EACH OF ITS FOUR LINES AS THE FIRST LINE
## OF FOUR POEMS IN REPLY

JAKUSHITSU GENKŌ, *TD* 81:104a

"Wise as a dragon, the sharp old priest in the mountains"?
Indeed, how could any mere mortal be so stubbornly eccentric?
This morning with a laugh I set out with a basket
To gather chestnuts I forget to peel before I eat!

> *The first line of Jakushitsu's poem repeats a line of the poem
> sent him by the monk Hōgai Genkei about 1320. The line can
> also be read "The sharp old priest of Ryūju Mountain"; "Ryūju"
> is the "mountain name" or general temple designation of what
> is now Eianji in Shizuoka Prefecture, a temple founded by
> Jakushitsu.*

## ARRIVING AT HAN-CHIA: SENT TO SHIH-CH'IAO

SESSON YŪBAI, *GBZS* I:536; *GBSS* III:873

A monk came searching to bring me your letter—
Ruining half a night's sleep here in this mountain hut,
A passing squall through the pines blew some rain by:
Now, through a broken window, the new moon climbs the shoulder of a
    peak.

## SENT TO THE MONK SEKIRYŌ OF SEIFUKUJI, OFF IN CHINA

MING-CHI CH'U-CHUN, *GBZS* III:2017

The distance between us must not be the measure of our closeness;
In both lands the scenery has turned to spring,
And we are both strangers in a strange land now,
The two of us lifting our broken begging-bowls.

## 14. Tea

Tea-drinking originated in China, but it was in Japan that it attained the status of an art. The start of tea-drinking in Japan is traditionally credited to Myōan Eisai, who returned from a trip to China in 1193 bringing with him a great many of the cultural achievements of the Sung dynasty including tea-plant seeds and a knowledge of the connoisseurship of tea-drinking.

Tea was used in the Zen temples at first for its power to keep meditating monks wakeful and able to concentrate, and also as a kind of tonic medicine that Eisai touted to his warrior patron as a remedy for hangover. During the fourteenth century, however, tea-drinking became a fad in the temples. From the simple *sarei* ceremony of offering a bowl of tea before the portrait of a Zen master or Patriarch with respect, the drinking of tea soon became an inseparable part of any gathering of monks, and a proscription against tea-parties began to take its place alongside the more traditional warnings posted at the temple gates forbidding meat, strong drink, and the like. The great Musō Soseki wrote that tea-drinking was useful when carried out in the context of the Zen monk's search for enlightenment; "The way it is done these days, however, it amounts to a performing art and is a detriment to the Way!"

---

### SIPPING TEA BEFORE THE BLOSSOMS

KISEI REIGEN, *GBSS* II:208

Each time these blossoms open I recall the friend who gave me the
    saplings,
And the times we used to stop to drink beneath his trees;
But those springs of twenty years ago are like a dream,
And the wine cups of those days are tea-bowls now.

## THE SOUND OF TEA BOILING

GAKUIN EKATSU, *GBZS* III:2664

Its thin song the wind springing up in distant valley pines,
Its roiling boil evening rain falling on a cold river;
A mind befuddled by the city temples' daily brawl
Hears this pure sound, and inner calm steeps in the deepening evening.

## THANKING KYŪHŌ AND KOTEN FOR THEIR GIFTS OF TEA

GIDŌ SHŪSHIN, *GBZS* II:1374 [498]

With a ladle-full of its clear flow I boil some icy stream—
How the lingering taste concentrates my divided mind!
Now a very lazy old man, greedy for his spring nap,
Is awake and alert enough to sit in meditation.

## NINTH DAY OF THE NINTH MONTH:
## RAIN—RHYMING WITH CHŪHO'S POEM
## "INSCRIBED AT THE PAVILION OF HORIZONTAL BAMBOOS"

GIDŌ SHŪSHIN, *GBZS* II:1389 [513]

Across the river in the green mountains the rain's half lifted,
But moss grows on the clogs I used to wear on former outings;
There's no more urge in my old self to go climb mountains any more—
I'll sit, roll up the thin blinds, and *pour* myself some green.

## BREWING TEA

BETSUGEN ENSHI, *GBZS* I:754

On clouds of jade green, drawn out on the breeze,
Stretch white blossoms over the bowl's surface, cooling to the touch;
As the mountain moon stirs plum-blossom shadows on the window,
I fill the rough bowl again, sip the lingering fragrance.

## 15. Animals

The Zen poets wrote about animals frequently, perhaps because stories about animals figure so often in collections of kōans. The first story in the *Mumonkan*, for example, deals with the question of whether or not a dog has Buddha-nature. Cats were an inevitable sight in the large Zen temples, clearly reflecting a need to keep up with hordes of mice and rats. It was theoretically improper for a Buddhist monk to take life, even of something as insignificant as a rat or a fly; but it was the nature of cats to eat rats, and there was no harm in allowing nature to take its course. Still, the monks occasionally wrote poems warning the mice not to engage in their pilfering quite so openly lest they be killed: the contradictions of life in the Gozan were manifold.

## MOURNING MY OLD CAT

MING-CHI CH'U-CHUN, *GBZS* III:1992

1

Here and in China we depended on one another these twenty years,
Sleeping in the same bed, sharing the same food;
But now that your soul has flown below to the Nine Springs,
The mice don't even bother to act crafty anymore.

2

With your godlike awe you pacified the mice so effectively
That I'm burying you in a coffin just as I would a person;
And, mindful of the story of Pai-chang's fox,
The ceremony will be carried out in strict accordance with the old ways.

> *The story of Pai-chang's fox appears as the second case in the*
> Mumonkan. *An old man who kept appearing at Pai-chang's*
> *lectures confided to the monk that he was not a human being,*
> *but a fox who was once a priest on the same mountain. Once,*
> *asked whether an enlightened man continued to remain subject*
> *to the chain of causality, he had answered in the negative, and*
> *so was doomed to suffer five hundred reincarnations in the form*
> *of a fox. Pai-chang, asked for an answer that could release him,*
> *declared that all beings are subject to the chain of cause and*
> *effect. The fox-creature was thereupon enlightened and told*
> *Pai-chang that he would find the body of a fox nearby, and*
> *requested that it be buried as a human.*

## LISTENING TO THE MICE CHEWING

NANKŌ SŌGAN, *GBSS* VI:256

They hide by day and come out at night—the thieves are hard to cope
   with,
Chewing away in the dark spaces; I get no response
When I rap underneath the bed with my hand, so
Pinching my nose I try some meows, imitating my calico cat.

## ON A FAN: PEONIES AND A SLEEPING CAT

KŌZEI RYŪHA, *GBSS* VII:192

The rascally kitten's forever mewing at its mother in hunger,
In constant complaint at my temple's wretched poverty,
But a mound of meat heaped his plate on this festival day—
Now, under the peonies, he sleeps in the spring sunshine.

## ASKING FOR KITTENS

SEIIN SHUNSHŌ, *GBZS* III:2768 [810]

These two kittens chewed your wisteria vines to death,
So you had the happy inspiration to send *me* the calico rascals?
It's not as if I had enough breakfast in my cold kitchen to share,
But it's better than Nan-ch'üan's crude solution!

> *Case 14 in the* Mumonkan *tells of the monk Nan-ch'üan returning to his temple to find two monks arguing over the ownership of a cat. Nan-ch'üan held the cat aloft and announced that if no one could say anything to make him spare the animal he would kill it with a knife. Ch'ao-chou, asked later what he would have done, said nothing but took off his sandals and put them on his head. Nan-ch'üan said to him, "If you had been here, the cat would still be alive."*

## SQUIRRELS

KOKAN SHIREN, *GBZS* I:154

Safe up there in the treetops you snicker at the cat,
As the nuts ripen under the frost on a thousand trees;
To forget about putting a violent end to your thieving hearts,
I'd have to have done zazen with old Yang-ch'i himself!

> *Yang-ch'i Fang-hui (996–1049) was the founder of the dominant southern line of Lin-ch'i (Rinzai) in the Sung, the line continued by Wu-chun Shih-fan and later in Japan by the Chinese priests Wu-hsüeh Tsu-yüan and Wu-an P'u-ning. Kokan's line was that of Enni Ben'en (Tōfukuji), who studied in China with Wu-chun.*

## 16. Illness and Death

There is really no need to say much about this unavoidable topic: illness was not the occasion for much Zen philosophy. Monks did write about the deaths of friends and masters, however. When a Zen monk died, according to the biographical convention, he did it on a day he had chosen beforehand, after writing a farewell poem to his disciples.

---

### WRITTEN WHILE ILL: A HUMOROUS POEM TO SHOW MY PUPILS

GIDŌ SHŪSHIN, *GBZS* II:1394 [518]

A hundred afflictions have taken their turn ravaging this leaky frame,
What's left of my life is already spent with ghosts for neighbors;
I really have to laugh at you silly children—
Trying to keep spring from leaving by clutching at blossoms in the air!

> *"Blossoms in the air" is a literal translation of Gidō's sobriquet* Kūge.

### WHILE ILL: WRITING MY THOUGHTS

KOKEN MYŌKAI, *GBZS* III:2093 [137]

My worn-out sandals hang high from the bare wall,
And dawn's brought spring snow that makes the blossoms open;
Those twenty years of pilgrimage I made in China?
Better to have slept here in this mountain hut.

## HUMOROUS POEM: A RHYMING ANSWER
## TO GIDEN'S POEM ON "EYE TROUBLES"

GIDŌ SHŪSHIN, *GBZS* II:1351 [475]

I hear since spring you've suffered from blurred vision,
And imagine you're too depressed to lift your head to the world—
But the sooner you understand that the "colors of the world are unreal,"
The sooner you'll look upon those "flowers in the mist" without distress.

> *The* Prajñāpāramitā Sutra *(Hannyakyō) contains the phrase* shiki
> soku ze kū, *"color is emptiness," meaning that the apparent
> individual physical manifestations of things in the world are an
> illusion.*

# IN CHINA: SICK WITH MALARIAL FEVER

CHŪGAN ENGETSU, *GBZS* II:866 [10]; *GBSS* IV:323

Every nasty bug has schemed to plague me with disease,
The twin Gods of Illness bore holes in my chest and diaphragm
("He's old—why not kill him off?"),
Send vermin of darkness to release their poisonous venom.
The suffocating heat of my body has steamed my vitality away,
I quake as though struck by thunder;
Heaven and earth have become a gigantic two-part steamer
And all the gravy pours out of me.
But suddenly comes a chill to chase away the heat,
And I shiver as though drowning under ice,
Pile up more blankets over coverlets and quilts,
No end to the number I can take.
Why, in such a brief span of time,
Do Yin and Yang alternate so violently?
I cough and I sneeze,
Tears running mixed with phlegm,
Toss and turn but can't find peace
No matter how I rearrange pillow and mattress;
I have trouble whether I'm up or down,
For the slightest movement someone must support me,
So dizzy I confuse square and round,
Fall over all the time, go black and blank out.
All my life I've eaten a vegetarian diet,
And it's always suited my taste just fine:
So the five whole mullet they've set before me now
Taste about as appetizing as frozen quinine bark.
In the short while I've been confined to this hammock,
My scrawny body has turned to jerky;
People passing by look in
Wondering if I'm not dead and just pretending to be alive.
All day groans issue from my mouth—
Whatever comes brings anger or terror.
Returning to consciousness, I compose myself:
A visitor from far across the seas,
No one knows my mind
Or has pity for a strange accent.

## MOURNING FOR MY MOTHER

RYŪSEN REISAI, *GBZS* I:584

Undone, in haggard disarray, no longer capable of composure,
My appearance expresses completely what I feel;
Wind sighs mournfully through sere, leafless mulberry trees—
How can there be so much grief in a wash of setting sun?

## TO RHYME WITH A POEM BY MY OLD TEACHER:
## SICK IN WINTER

RYŪSEN REISAI, *GBZS* I:609

Driven against the paper windows, flying sleet borne on a sour wind;
Sitting on a mat, hanging lamp left unlit, I watch the desolate scene.
The sound of a dark brown hungry rat overturning a stoneware jar
Strikes my ears like the knelling of a bell.

> *The poem alludes to case seven of the* Mumonkan *in which the
> sound of a bell is equated with truth, that of a stoneware jar
> with delusion.*

# BIOGRAPHIES OF THE POETS

## Banri Shūkyū (1428–1502)

Banri was originally trained at Tōfukuji but moved to Shōkokuji at the age of fifteen—an almost unheard-of change of faction in a period of extreme factional partisanship. After Shōkokuji was burned to the ground by marauding soldiers, he fled to Ōmi in 1467 and in 1469 moved to Minō and in 1470 to Owari. By this time he had drifted quite far from his original affiliation with the monks of the Tōfukuji line, associating mainly with the Shōkokuji monks of Musō Soseki's instead. It was not long before the Tōfukuji faction revealed its displeasure. Caught in the middle, Banri took what seemed the next logical step in a direction that was becoming increasingly clear, and abandoned monastic life altogether to return to lay life.

There were varying reactions among the Gozan monks to the upsetting years of the Ōnin Wars (1467–77). Some fled into reclusiveness, never again to return to Kyoto and the world of the major temples. For others like Ikkyū Sōjun and Nankō Sōgan, the times were just another stage in what they regarded as the increasingly rapid slide of the Gozan into final and total depravity; they had already abandoned the Zen establishment well before the Ōnin years. In Banri's case the monk was apparently already sufficiently inclined toward the lay life that, when surprised by civil war, he reacted by simply allowing himself to drift into a way of life that did not permit him to remain a monk. Indeed, by 1472 he was already married and had two children (Senri and Hyakuri), although he did not yet live with his family, but rather in temples belonging to Musō's faction. In 1480 he finally built a retreat within a temple in Minō where he settled with his family.

Banri maintained an active role in the literary side of temple life, which may have been in fact the greater side by this time. His expenses were borne in part by the temple and in part by lay patrons for whom he played the role of poetry teacher and professional literary advisor—a life indistinguishable from those led by the professional dōbōshū ("aesthetic advisors" to the Shogun and the daimyos) and renga masters of the day. By 1482 Banri had completed work on a voluminous annotated edition of the Sung poet Su Shih's collected works that is still extant and one of the primary sources for the study of late Muromachi Japanese. Banri was paid to lecture on this work, an activity that became his primary support in life.

In 1485, at the invitation of a friend, the warrior-poet Ōta Dōkan (1432–86), Banri left Minō for Edo Castle to be in attendance on the daimyo Uesugi Sadamasa (1442–93), Dōkan's liege lord. With such powerful support Banri would be able to devote full time to cultivating his new role of *suki* or professional man of taste. He soon found himself so comfortably settled that he summoned his family to Edo. Several of the poems translated in this volume date from the period of his journey to Edo in 1485, and the poems in his collection are carefully dated and annotated by Banri himself.

In 1486 Banri's patron Ōta was assassinated by Uesugi on the basis of some rumor. Banri tried to leave Edo at once, but found himself detained forcibly in Edo with little to do and less inclination to do it. He was finally given permission in 1488 to depart for Minō, staying for a time en route at the military camp of the son of his former patron. During this unhappy return journey, Banri was accompanied by an entourage composed of his wife and children, monks, attendants, and at least one concubine. The poems he wrote on the trip back to Minō are, in spite of the experiences of the years and the unsettled circumstances of his life, remarkably less misanthropic than those he had written on the road to Edo. Indeed, one would be hard pressed to find any writer who appears to have been as disenchanted with the common folk as Banri. This intolerant side of his personality may have been a factor in his eventual decision to abandon monastic life.

Banri's poems became progressively more eccentric as he grew older, often written in a "Chinese" so Japanese that it sometimes seems a sort of pidgin, fraught with literary allusions that refer more frequently to Japanese sources than to Chinese.

### Betsugen Enshi (1294–1364)

Betsugen spent the ten years between 1320–1330 studying in China under the master Ku-lin Ch'ing-mao (1262–1329), a famous Ch'an monk visited by nearly every Japanese who studied in China during his lifetime. Among those whose works appear in this volume, for example, Jakushitsu Genkō, Chūgan Engetsu, Koken Myōkai, and Tesshū Tokusai sought him out. Ku-lin was also the teacher of Chu-hsien Fan-hsien, an important Chinese priest who arrived in Japan in 1330.

Ku-lin himself wrote that he had high regard for Betsugen and expected much of him. He gave Betsugen his seal of enlightment (*inka*) in 1325. Still another Chinese monk wrote in a preface of 1322 that Betsugen's Chinese was so excellent that he "could be mistaken for a Korean." One scholar has estimated that the number of Japanese and Korean monks in China at this time exceeded that of Chinese. The praise cited above would seem to indicate that the linguistic talents of the Koreans were apparently thought by the Chinese to be superior to those of Japanese.

In spite of this apparently warm reception by the Chinese, Betsugen seems to have been nearly always depressed during his stay, if we accept the evidence of his poetry. The collection of his poetry written while in China, the *Nan'yūshū* ("Collection of a Southern Journey"), is full of poems addressed to Japanese monks expressing his homesickness.

Following his return to Japan in 1330, Betsugen spent twenty years living far from the two centers of power, Kyoto and Kamakura, in small temples along the Japan Sea coast. He even declined the offer of the abbacy of Nanzenji in Kyoto once, apparently determined, like Jakushitsu Genkō, to live out his life in the provinces. In the last year of his life, however, old and infirm at seventy-one, Betsugen was summoned by the Shogun Ashikaga Yoshiakira to head Kenninji in Kyoto; as if to justify his worst fears, death arrived shortly after he was forced to take up his duties there.

### Chūgan Engetsu (1300–1375)

One month after Chūgan's birth his father was sent into exile in Shikoku and the child was abandoned by the mother, passed on from a nurse to a grandfather, left with a grandmother, taken to a temple in Kamakura, and soon passed on to another temple. The rest of his life seems to flow naturally from this inauspicious beginning. "Because of his wretched childhood, he would respond eagerly to anyone that was nice to him—so eagerly, in fact, that would-be patrons soon tired of him and chased him off. He seems almost paranoid in his belief that others were out to get him—and with some justification."* Indeed, although Chūgan possessed a gift for composing striking poetry, rather neatly ordered with nice, parallel antitheses, he often seemed to fail wretchedly at nearly everything else.

At seventeen Chūgan began study under a Chinese priest, Tung-ming Hui-jih (Tōmei E'nichi, who arrived in Japan in 1308 and died 1340), a priest of the Sōtō Zen sect, and of the single Sōtō line in Japan that differed from that of its Japanese founder Dōgen. Another of Tōmei's students was Betsugen Enshi.

In 1318, Chūgan left Kamakura for Hakata in Kyushu, where all ships for China departed. The fixed number of monks permitted on the next ship had already been reached, however, and Chūgan was not to get to the mainland until 1325. In the meanwhile, he returned twice to Kamakura to take up study with Tōmei, was shown favor by the influential monk Kokan Shiren in Kyoto, and even met a future patron, Ōtomo Sadamune of Hakata.

*See Tamamura Takeji, *GBSS* IV:1221.

Once in China, Chūgan studied with Ku-lin Ch'eng-mao, the Chinese master best known to the Japanese at that time. By 1328, he tried to return to Japan, but failed to get on a ship. Hearing that his Japanese friend Fumon Kaimon (1302–1369) had been imprisoned, Chūgan set out to try to rescue him. By the time he arrived on the scene, however, Fumon had already been released. In 1330 Chūgan studied with the famous Chinese master Tung-yang Te-hui for a year and made the rounds of several teachers before finally returning to Japan in 1332.

In 1339, just when all seemed to be going well, Chūgan had a disastrous falling-out with his old teacher Tung-ming, and announced in Kyoto that he would follow Tung-yang's line instead, even though he had studied with him in China for only a year. When he returned to Kamakura his old friends turned on him, and it is recorded that one monk even set upon him with a sword. The year 1342 found Chugan searching for a ship back to China—perhaps with the intention of remaining for good—but he was prohibited from leaving Japan.

From the time of the death of his patron Ōtomo in 1333, Chūgan had held a titular position as head of the clan's temple in Kyushu. In 1345, the main statue was stolen from the temple, and Chūgan spent a great deal of time traveling in search of it. In 1347 he began to teach in another Ōtomo-sponsored temple in a mountainous region in the provinces, but lost the job in 1348 because of a power-struggle in the Ōtomo clan. After Chūgan had spent several wretched years in the provinces things started to look up. He was introduced to Ashikaga Tadayoshi in Kamakura in 1351, and two years later was given his first major post, the abbacy of Manjuji in Kamakura and then of Manjuji in Kyoto, a Gozan temple, and of Kenninji in 1360.

On the fifteenth of the twelfth month, 1362 a monk shot an arrow at Chūgan. It missed, but the incident precipitated an attack of paranoia that ended in a nervous breakdown in 1364. One of the symptoms was an unfortunate tendency to laugh at the wrong times. Chūgan eventually recovered to head Nanzenji in 1370 and the recently burned-down Tenryūji in 1373.

In 1375, when he was on the point of death at seventy-six, his disciples begged him for the customary last poem. Chūgan only replied that he had already said too much, and told them to go away.

### Gakuin Ekatsu (1351–1425)

Gakuin Ekatsu began his Zen study with Zekkai Chūshin in 1379. He went to China in 1386, returning to Japan in 1395 where he lived in temples belonging to Musō Soseki's line in Shikoku until 1410 when he was made abbot of Shōkokuji, by then the most powerful of the Kyoto Gozan. After heading several other major temples, he returned to Shōkokuji in

1425 to found the sub-temple Chōtoku-in. The official account of his life records that Zekkai passed on a robe of Musō's to him as a special mark of favor and honor.

The largest number of his poems, in the eight-line *lü-shih* form, seem undistinguished, but his four-line *chüeh-chü* poems are among the finest produced by the Gozan monks.

### Gidō Shūshin (1325–1388)

While Musō Soseki was unquestionably the central figure in Gozan political history, it is his two disciples Gidō Shūshin and Zekkai Chūshin who have come to be regarded as the "twin pillars" of Gozan literature. Gidō was said to excel in poetry, Zekkai in prose.

While it is certain that Gidō exerted a profound influence on the course of Gozan letters, a close examination of his voluminous poetry fails to bear out his reputation on literary grounds alone. A significant part of that reputation rests on the somewhat exaggerated praise given his poems by Chinese literati and monks that is so carefully chronicled in Gidō's own diary, the *Kūge Nichiyō Kufū Shū*, an important source document in medieval history.

Even more of his reputation rests on the crucial role Gidō played in his relations with the Shogun Yoshimitsu and the Regent Nijō Yoshimoto while Gidō was in Kyoto in the last eight years of his life. What remains of his fame unaccounted for by these elements may be attributed to his poetry, and even then not so much to its high quality as to the overwhelmingly social nature of his extant 1,739 poems, so frequently occasional. It would appear that nearly every contemporary monk of any importance—and many of little importance at all—received at least one of his ubiquitous farewells, congratulations, laments, notes, jokes or the like on some occasion. By far the greater number of his poems contain little literary merit apart from skillful puns on the names of monks and temples (a literary form practiced by nearly all Gozan poets). The most enjoyable of his poems are the "fan inscriptions," short poems inscribed on fans that beautifully capture the essence of a moment. The genre of poetry intended to grace paintings on fans or scrolls began in Japan in this period, and Gidō's are so good that one feels sorry that he trivialized his talent by squandering it on trifles. In a preface dated 1382, Gidō in his later years repented having done so himself.

While Gidō's poetry is fundamentally courtly and aristocratic in tone, he was widely read in Chinese literary criticism, and was instrumental in introducing central Chinese literary concepts into contemporary discussion of literary theory in Japan, mainly through his influence on Yoshimoto. Gidō discussed literature with the Regent as a "bait" to draw him and the Shogun into a deeper understanding of Zen, exactly as

Gidō's teacher Musō Soseki had done with Ashikaga Takauji and Tada-yoshi and with Reizei Tamesuke. Like Musō too, Gidō never went to China—an omission that, curiously, seems to have been almost requisite in his day for membership in the mainstream of the Gozan, which was rapidly growing more Japanese in its orientation.

Gidō's diary records some thirty meetings with Nijō Yoshimoto be-tween 1380 and 1386. Gidō was always hoping to teach the Regent more about Zen, but privately thought him hopelessly mired in mundane con-cerns, and constantly stressed to him the idea, derived from Chinese lit-erary thought, of transcendence of the mundane (*zoku*). Yoshimoto, for his part, repeated Gidō's ideas on literary theory verbatim in important theoretical works like the *Kyūshū Mondō*. It seems odd that Gidō could draw as clear a distinction as he did between his own prolific literary activities, writing poetry that often appears very un-Zen-like; and the activities of Yoshimoto, who was often at pains to attempt to reconcile his own literary activities with Buddhist theory.

Gidō suffered all his life from badly blurred vision probably caused by cataracts, and took the sobriquet of Kūge, which can mean both "spots in the air" or "flowers of emptiness." The expression comes from the *Laṅkāvatāra Sūtra*: "It is like a person with a cataract who sees spots in the air—when the cataract is removed, the spots disappear." Dōgen had used the expression in *Shōbōgenzō* as an image of delusion; Gidō turned his eye troubles into a positive source of enlightenment, feeling that his deceptive eyes kept pointing up the illusory nature of what oth-ers accepted as "reality," and wrote the following Zen poem on his name:

> Emptiness without form,
> Flowers without fruit—
> Only those who can see these
> May enter my temple.
> GBZS II:1899

### Ishō Tokugan (1360–1437)

Most Zen monks were taken to temples while still very young. Ishō Tokugan was unaccountably born in one in Kyushu, going to Nanzenji in Kyoto at sixteen. From 1377 he traveled extensively from one provincial temple to another, and by 1385 he was made head of Chōrakuji in the province of Settsu. He later spent three years at the largest of the tem-ples in Kamakura, returning to Kyoto in 1397. By 1411, after careful advancement through the ranks of the Gozan system, he was made head of Manjuji in Kyoto, returning to Nanzenji in 1413. He became head of Tenryūji in 1421, retiring almost immediately to devote the remainder of his life to letters.

Ishō is said to have been the only monk besides Zekkai Chūshin who could actually think in Chinese. Like Zekkai too, Ishō was known as a contrary person (one scholar has even described Zekkai's entire line as "cranky").* Ishō was considered one of the greatest Japanese experts on the poetry of Su Tung-p'o, and one of his commentaries on Su's poetry is still extant. His own poems are full of obscure and arcane lines and of the complex Taoist imagery of hermetic withdrawal from the world and its concerns.

### Jakushitsu Genkō (1290–1367)

Jakushitsu was born into a noble Fujiwara family said to have been descended from Ono Saneyori, a Regent during the reign of Emperor Murakami (r. 946–967). After studying at Nanzenji between 1317 and 1319 with its abbot, the Chinese priest I-shan I-ning, Jakushitsu spent the years 1321–26 in China. He seems to have managed to avoid the problems experienced by Sesson Yūbai who was in China at the same time, and never ran afoul of the Mongol authorities. The two Japanese visited many of the same masters.

After returning to Japan, Jakushitsu spent the next thirty-six years in a succession of unimportant provincial temples in a self-imposed hermitage away from the centers of power. When offered the abbacy of Tenryūji in 1362 and of Kenchōji the next year—two of the most important Gozan temples—he turned the posts down, apparently afraid he might die in a city temple rather than in the wilderness he had come to love.

Jakushitsu's hermitic spirit reaches into his poetry and is its informing element. His poems seem fresh, even raw, with a muscularity that is relatively scarce in the poetry of his contemporaries.

### Kakua (1143–?)

Kakua was a monk of the Tendai Enryakuji temple complex located on Mt. Hiei to the northeast of Kyoto. He went to China in 1171, near the end of the Heian period, and studied with the famous Lin-Ch'i master Hsia-t'ang Hui-yüan (1103–1176) at Ling-yin-ssu temple near modern Hangchou.

Kakua was only one of the many Japanese priests who went to China at this time interested primarily in the study of T'ien-T'ai (Tendai) and Chen-yen (Shingon) Buddhism, and like many others only became interested in Zen after arriving in China, where the sect was flourishing.

His poems translated here have been called examples of the earliest

*Tamamura Takeji in *GBSS* II:1288.

Buddhist hymns (*ge*) written by Japanese using a specifically Zen vocabulary.*

### Keijō Shūrin (1440–1518)

Keijo was brought to Shōkokuji Temple to be raised at the age of five. His early training included the Chinese literary classics which, according to an anecdote in his recorded deeds, he was forced to con verbatim or suffer a beating for every word missed. His literary training was continued by Ōsen Keisan, and from the age of sixteen Keijo attended gatherings of *renku* and *wakan renku* (linked verse composed in Chinese, or in Chinese and Japanese) along with his mentor.

After heading several large temples, Keijo was given an appointment as Envoy to China (a post always given to Gozan monks) by the government in 1490. He declined the position, however. His friend Kisen Shūshō alleged in a diary entry that Keijo was not cut out for political life, for he was sickly from birth, and, "being constantly preoccupied with literary concerns such as writing sermons, reading books and composing poetry, his natural bent is toward wit, not diplomacy."

Keijo was made abbot of Shōkokuji in 1495 and *Sōroku* or chief executive officer of the Gozan the next year, in which post he remained until 1504. He returned to the headship of Shōkokuji again in 1506, and died in that temple in 1518. From his diary entries as *Sōroku* it is clear that Keijo's role as advisor to the Shogun Yoshizumi (r. 1493–1508) was concerned mainly with trying to moderate the Shogun's excessive fondness for drink, theatricals, and boys.

Nearly three-quarters of Keijo's voluminous poetry is composed of inscriptions on paintings and fans, and its very strong visual quality derives from this association with ink-painting. The sheer quantity of these poems indicates that Keijo was considered among artists as something of a professional writer of such inscriptions, and his poems were valued as perfect complements to the ink-paintings of his contemporaries.

Keijo's rather idiosyncratic usage of the Chinese language may have been among the factors in his refusing the post of Envoy to Ming China. His Chinese often smacks of Japanese in lexicon and grammatical usage, and in fact is sometimes best interpreted by simply reading it in Japanese word-order and with Japanese in mind. This shortcoming (as it was referred to by his Zen contemporaries) may be less an individual anomaly than an indication of the degree to which even the Sinified world of the Gozan was being influenced by the powerful forces of assimilation of things Chinese into the mainstream of Japanese culture, forces which reached their peak during Keijo's lifetime.

*See Tamura Takeji, *Gozan Bungaku* (Tokyo: Shibundō, 1955), 56–57.

### Kisei Reigen (1403–1488)

Kisei was a precocious poet, a child prodigy invited while in his early teens to poetry gatherings at the Imperial Palace in Kyoto. He was adopted as the son of the powerful *kanrei* (deputy regent) Hosokawa Mitsumoto in 1409, it being a custom of the period for powerful warriors to take young monks as adopted sons. Because of his adoption, Kisei made a point all his life of refusing any and all advancement in the temple world. He chose instead to remain at the extraordinarily humble post of *jisha* or "attendant" until the time of his death because, as a Hosokawa protégé, it would have been wise to avoid the risks of inevitable involvement in Ashikaga politics that prominence in the Gozan entailed; and the course of political events culminating in the Ōnin War proved him right. Kisei made his choice of career while quite young: he was at the Hosokawa residence at the age of seven when he was first seen there by the Shogun Yoshimochi, who asked Kisei whether the lad regarded himself or Hosokawa as his father. Kisei replied that he thought of Hosokawa as a father, and thus the die was cast.

Kisei was sent by his patron to study with the most eminent of the Gozan poet-monks of the time, Kōzei Ryūha, and a large part of his subsequent training was in the composition of poetry. Following Hosokawa Mitsumoto's death in 1427, Kisei elected to devote himself to the life of a low-ranking monk and scholar, and in fulfillment of his vow he would turn down offers of the highest offices to which a Zen monk could attain.

Kisei was the earliest of the Gozan monks whose poetry is translated here to live through the upheavals of the Ōnin Wars that began in 1467 and continued for a period of eleven years, by the end of which nearly every temple and public building in Kyoto had been reduced to charred rubble. Monks fled to the countryside temples of warrior patrons—if they had them—helping in their dispersal to disseminate a fair amount of the high culture of the metropolitan temples throughout Japan. Kisei's own patrons, the Hosokawas, were ranged on one side of the conflict, and Kisei was able to retreat to a temple supported by them in the valleys of Tamba not far to the west of Kyoto. When events in the capital permitted him to return, along with most of the Gozan monks after the worst of the fighting in 1469, Kisei took up residence in another Hosokawa-sponsored temple in Kyoto, ending his days at Nanzenji. One scholar has suggested that Kisei was the vital bridge in the literature and scholarship of the Kitayama era that preceded, and the Higashiyama era that followed, the Ōnin Wars.*

---

*Imaeda Aishin, "Gozan gakugei shijō ni okeru Kisei Reigen no rekishiteki chii—Kitayama yori Higashiyama e," *Kokushigaku* (January 1951), 35–47.

### Kōhō Kennichi (1241–1316)

Kōhō was a son of Emperor Go-Saga. He began study with the Chinese priest Wu-hsüeh Tsu-yüan at the relatively advanced age of sixteen, having first received a thoroughly Japanese education appropriate to the son of royalty. His poems translated here are examples of the sort of *waka* poetry written by Gozan monks that comprises a tiny but significant part of the history of Gozan literature.

Kōhō was not the first Zen monk to write poetry in Japanese, though few in fact did, brushing off all letters in Japanese as "not our business." Earlier Zen monks such as Eisai and Dōgen, trained as Tendai monks and in close contact with the Kyoto nobility, also wrote in Japanese as well as Chinese, the language of the Gozan. Many of Kōhō's poems were included in the Imperial Anthologies *Fūgashū* and *Shinzoku Kokin Wakashū*, and his *waka* were compiled in a private collection by the well-known fifteenth-century waka poet Kazan'in Nagachika. His poems are thoroughly of their time in diction and allusion.

Kōhō is best remembered as the teacher of Musō Soseki, in whom he instilled a taste for and skill in waka poetry. He never wanted his words preserved on paper, but had to wait 250 years to get his wish: Toyotomi Hideyoshi burned down Unganji in Kai province, the temple that contained his records, on the grounds that an enemy had taken refuge there.

### Kokan Shiren (1278–1345)

Kokan was best known in his own day, and is still remembered today, for his history of Buddhism in Japan, *Genkō Shakusho* (1322); in the poem translated here as "Himself," Kokan remarks that "Complier of the *History of the Monks*" was among the "evil names" he had earned. The work, the first history of Buddhism written in Japan, was prompted by Kokan's acute sense of shame when his teacher, the Chinese monk I-shan I-ning (Issan Ichinei, 1247–1317), arriving in Japan in 1299, asked to peruse a history of the sect there and found there was none.

Always sickly since childhood, Kokan showed precocious talents as a scholar and became known for his scholarship from an early age. He never went to China. His disciple Shōkai Reiken, returning to Japan in 1351 after twelve years there making the rounds of the most famous masters, stated flatly that he never found a better teacher than Kokan (*GBZS* II:1254).

Kokan developed the syncretic study of neo-Confucianism and Zen that was initiated in Sung China and first brought to Japan by Enni Ben'en, the founder of Kokan's Tōfukuji faction, of which Kokan became head when he assumed the abbacy of the temple in 1332. Kokan's interpretation emphasized an eclectic notion of "maturity" attained through practice in learning *li* (Japanese *ri*, the natural innate principles of things, a fundamental concept of neo-Confucian philosophy) from the "observation of things." The result of the conscientious application of his theory in practice is revealed in hundreds of small poems on insignificant, everyday subjects such as squirrels, mosquitoes, earthquakes, baths and the like, the *li* of which he sought to epitomize in poetry. While Kokan denied any particular talent for poetry and had little confidence in his own, his poems bear up well in comparison with those written by other Gozan monks.

### Koken Myōkai (?–ca. 1390)

Koken entered Tenryūji when young to study with Musō Soseki. He went to China between 1345 and 1365, returning to Tenryūji. In 1383 he was appointed abbot of Kenninji in Kyoto, another Gozan temple, and later became head of Kenchōji of Kamakura.

Koken is best known in the history of the Gozan as the author of a letter of 1378 appealing the Shogun to have Rinsenji (near Tenryūji in Saga, both founded by Musō), recently elevated to Gozan status under terms unacceptable to one group of Musō's followers, returned to its former status on the grounds that such unwarranted expansion would prove ruinous to Musō's line. The "Rinsenji incident" was only one small reflection of the bitter factional feuding that was already breaking out among Musō's followers a quarter-century after the Master's death.

### Kōzei Ryūha (1375–1446)

The word *kōzei* (Chinese *chiang-hsi*) suggests Ryūha's fundamental literary allegiance to a school of Chinese poets that followed the style of poetry of Huang T'ing-chien, known in Chinese as the founder of the Chiang-hsi school. Huang and Su Tung-p'o were the two Chinese poets most highly revered by the Gozan poets. The names of Ishō Tokugan and Kōzei Ryūha were often linked by Gozan critics in much the same manner as those of Su and Huang; but a late fifteenth-century Japanese annotator of the famous Chinese collection of Ch'an poetry *Chiang-hu Feng-yüeh Chi* ("Collected Poems of Zen Monks") denied any such resemblance with the comment that while the poets Su and Huang were "real Zen masters," the Zen monks Ishō and Kōzei were "mere Confucians."

With Kōzei, the idea that "poetry *is* Zen" was to become the representative formulation of the relationship between these two practices in the Gozan. Monks of the preceding generation like Gidō Shūshin had been careful to place poetry in a subordinate position to Zen practice, at least in theory, whatever their actual inclinations might have been. In Gidō's many apologiae on this issue, it is clear that he felt that as a Zen monk anything he might do, including poetry, was by definition Zen. Kōzei, however, made his case even more uncompromisingly: "There is no Zen outside of poetry, and no poetry outside of Zen."

One scholar finds in Kōzei's poetry the overwrought style of the late T'ang poets like Li Shang-yin, and in his diction the disjointed constructions of Tu Fu. This seems exaggerated; but whatever the actual case, it is true that later Gozan poets traced either a strain of "strange beauty" or one of "dissipation"—depending on their point of view—back to the poetry of Kōzei.

Kōzei's career reached a critical point in 1422 when he was forty-seven years old. Apparently slandered by a group within Musō's faction out of jealousy (that faction had by this time grown so enormous that the single label hardly does it justice), he departed Kyoto under a cloud, and did not return for three years. Even after his return to Kyoto he was out of favor with the government, and kept out of sight until the death of the Shogun Yoshimochi in 1428. After the Shogun's death, Kōzei's career took a dramatic turn for the better. He seems to have been very concerned with ambitions in the Gozan world, and his main text in poetry was a sense of frustration and sadness at his failures, with the consolation of wine always near at hand.

### Lan-hsi Tao-lung (Rankei Dōryū, 1213–1278)

A Japanese priest, Getsu'ō Chikuyō of Sen'yūji in Kyoto, went to study in China, met Lan-hsi, and convinced him to come to Japan. Lan-hsi arrived in Japan in 1246 along with two other Chinese monks, the first Chinese to teach Zen in Japan.

After gaining the patronage of the Regent Hōjō Tokiyori (1227–63), Lan-hsi was made head of a temple in 1248 and of the newly completed Kenchōji in Kamakura in 1252. Except for the period between 1261–65, when he was unaccountably banished to a remote province on the basis of rumors that he was a Chinese spy, Lan-hsi continued to receive one honor after another from the Kamakura shogunate and headed several of the most important temples in Japan.

### Ming-chi Ch'u-chun (Minki Soshun, 1264–1336)

Ming-chi and Chu-hsien Fan-hsien, another Chinese Ch'an monk, both arrived in Japan in 1330, accompanied by the Japanese Zen monk Tengan Ekō. Since Ming-chi died six years after reaching Japan, and says in "Mourning My Old Cat" (p. 136) that he had had the animal for twenty years, we must suppose that he brought it with him all the way from China. The cat's name was "Abbot Hsiang-shan," named perhaps after the T'ang poet Po Chü-i (or else the temple of that name that Po adopted as his sobriquet). Sung poetry seems to abound in eulogies to cats, undoubtedly reflecting a need to keep up with hordes of rats and mice.

In the brief six years in Japan before his death Ming-chi seems never to have learned much Japanese. In the first two poems to a patron, Ōtomo Sadamune, he wrote

> I came ten thousand leagues over the seas to these shores
> Knowing nothing of the language that people here spoke:
> All I could make out was a babble of "bababa,"
> Couldn't catch more than something like "lilili."

Communication was effected through the medium of an expedient known as *hitsuwa* or "brush-talk," writing taking the place of conversation:

> To communicate my feelings, I took up a brush to say what was
>     on the tip of my tongue,
> And you caught my ideas by listening to my words with your
>     eyes. . . .

GBZS III:2026

For all his professed difficulty with the language, however, Ming-chi's poetry often sounds surprisingly Japanese. In "Start of Summer," for example, he frets as irritably over the uncertain weather that characterizes the rainy season in Japan as any Japanese *waka* poet did. Chinese poets seem to have been much less disposed to do this—not that coastal China does not have much the same weather in the same season, but perhaps because the enormous land mass of China experiences so many different weather patterns over the same span of time that a particular attitude toward any particular climatic phenomenon did not develop as easily as it did in the relatively tiny and much more homogeneous Japanese islands. Also, the attitudes of the Chinese toward seasonal change developed their classical literary expression in inland areas where there is less climatic variation than along the coast.

### Mugan Soō (?-1374)

Mugan never went to China to study, an omission increasingly common among the Japanese monks from the second half of the fourteenth century. He was in the line of Enni Ben'en at Tōfukuji in Kyoto, but after a promising start in the temple hierarchy, Mugan, like Jakushitsu Genkō and Betsugen Enshi, spent a very long period in the provinces at small temples, beginning in 1350. He was called to the abbacy of Tōfukuji in 1369; unlike other Gozan temples, Tōfukuji maintained the practice of recruiting its abbots exclusively from within its own ranks.

While he lived in the countryside, Mugan often wrote poetry on themes dealing with the lives of the peasants. Zen in theory and in ideal practice was not a salvationary creed, ignoring the spiritual needs of the common people for the patronage of the aristocracy and military classes. But in small country parishes away from the great centers of power, Zen priests were often called upon to provide the same pietistic services for the peasants that monks of the Jōdo and other Amidist sects were expected to contribute. In the long poem translated here, "Praying for an Abundant Harvest," Mugan details in a clearly uneasy and unsympathetic manner the customary annual visit to his temple by the local peasantry, deferential to the Zen priest but somewhat suspicious of him.

### Musō Soseki (1275–1351)

Musō is regarded as the most important figure in the history of medieval Japanese Zen, not so much for the influence or originality of his thought, but rather because of a personal character and style of Zen that guaranteed the perpetuation of the Zen establishment in Japan during the particularly difficult transition between the period of the Northern and Southern Courts and the early Muromachi period (that is, between 1330 and 1350). He gained the patronage of the powerful Ashikaga shoguns for the Zen sect, as well as their personal family allegiance to his own line—a line that includes most of the poets in this volume who lived after Musō.

Musō was of noble birth, a Genji probably distantly related to the ninth-century Emperor Uda. His aristocratic origins help to explain an early training in Tendai and Shingon Buddhism. Musō was also related to the Ashikagas by birth, being a maternal great-grandson of a daughter of Ashikaga Yoriuji (1189–1254).

When Musō was nineteen, a beloved teacher suffered a stroke that left the older man completely unable to read or write. Musō later wrote that it was this traumatic event that gave him his first impulse toward Zen. Yet at the same time, Musō appears to have been almost by nature unsuited to Zen, although events and choices he made propelled him along the path of Zen study. This conflict both symbolizes and exacerbated a personality that appears profoundly dualistic, alternating between extremes of withdrawal and involvement, belief and skepticism, Zen and Tendai-Shingon practice.*

The single most important event in Musō's later training was his abject failure under the Chinese master I-shan I-ning (Issan Ichinei), whose personal style of Zen was the rigorous Chinese style maintained in the Kamakura Gozan, and his subsequent enlightenment in 1305 under Kōhō Kennichi, whose similar background and style of Zen Musō found more congenial.

Following a period of withdrawal to mountain temples around Kamakura between 1312–18, Musō found himself in the first of a series of politically difficult and dangerous situations which he was to navigate

---

*Tamamura Takeji, *Musō Kokushi* (Kyoto: Sara Shobō, 1978), 26.

*Portrait of Musō Soseki*

with great caution and skill. Between 1320 and 1325 he had been made head of Nanzenji in Kyoto twice and of Engakuji in Kamakura once, remaining in his post only briefly before running off into hiding whenever he thought he could safely leave. He even once refused the abbacy of Kenchōji in Kamakura. He was constantly hounded by would-be disciples who, he complained, seemed to build villages of huts near him as soon as he thought he had found some remote mountain fastness. Finally, at the invitation of the Ashikagas, Musō founded Tenryūji in the Arashiyama area in the west of Kyoto in 1339.

When he had been in the throes of a personal crisis in 1303, Musō had appealed frantically to I-shan for encouragement and answers to his questions. The Chinese monk had only replied, in the best Zen manner, "There is no word, no Law, that I can give you." When Musō begged him for "compassion, some expedient," I-shan's only answer was, "No compassion, no expedients!" Musō would never become fond of the traditional Zen techniques of refusal, paradox, shouts and blows. Rather, his own style of Zen is chatty, affable, simple and accommodating, qualities that helped make it attractive to Japan's new Ashikaga rulers, provincial warriors without much sophistication in Zen, but with aspirations to aristocratic culture and ready to learn. The many existing portraits and statues of Musō reveal a gentle-looking man of extremely courtly bearing, almost comical with his long face and pointed dome and looking as though he would not harm a fly, in contrast to the ferocious, awesome and serious faces that so often scowl out from such likenesses.

Aspiring to the trappings of the aristocratic culture that they had only recently gained by force, the Ashikagas enjoyed the literary gatherings with Musō at Saihōji in Arashiyama where they could exchange *waka* poetry with him and be instructed—gently and simply—in Zen. Musō's compilation of their fictional "dialogs" comprises the text of the *Mūchū Mondō*, a work that is revealing in its degree of syncretism and its willing adaptation of Zen to the needs of the ruling class. It is extremely doubtful that the Ashikagas would have bothered much with any monk who insisted on bewildering them with Zen riddles and Chinese poetry.

Musō called his technique of teaching that of "calling the maid," a technique earlier elaborated by the Sung Dynasty monk Ta-hui Tsungkao (1089–1163); the Chinese expression, originally from a love poem, signified a woman who called to her maid, not because she required attention but because she wanted indirectly to make her lover aware of her presence. The expression thus means to hint indirectly at what one wants to say. Musō's use of poetry and simple, attractive teachings were designed to appeal to an untutored audience. While he frequently cited Ta-hui's strictures against literary involvement, he seems to have realized that it was precisely Ta-hui's own voluminous literature expounding

Ch'an for the benefit of the Chinese upper classes that made him the most popular monk in China in his day.†

### Nankō Sōgan (1397–1463)

Nankō Sōgan is a curious figure, an eccentric much like his well-known teacher Ikkyū Sōjun (1394–1481). Little is known of Nankō's life beyond the simple facts that he began his study of Zen at Shōkokuji and returned to lay life in later years, no doubt as disgusted with the entire Zen establishment as Ikkyū had been.

A long series of poems dealing with various Chinese poets indicates that Nankō was well-versed in mainland poetry. His own poetry consists in large part of the *enka* or "love poem" type, modeled after the style of the late T'ang poets that was popular in his day. Most of the poems included here date from his earlier years.

His poems are unusual in the number of Buddhist terms they contain. The clumsy Chinese phonetic renderings of Sanskrit words were assiduously avoided in poetry by Chinese and Japanese monks alike as "reeking of pickled vegetables"—a Chinese phrase used to indicate poetry that sounded too religiously monk-like, pickled vegetables constituting the major part of the monks' diet. To Nankō, however, the use of such words in poetry demonstrated greater transcendence of form since they prevented the poems from falling into worldly sentimentality and the sort of suggestive innuendo that was so popular at this time.

Nankō's long and scornful poem on the *odori nembutsu* or "Leaping Invocation of the Buddha's Name" offers an unusual glimpse into the lives of the lower classes, with whom the Zen sect had little to do on the whole as it catered rather to the spiritual and cultural needs of its ruling-class warrior patrons. The *odori nembutsu*, practiced by the believers of the pietistic sects of Buddhism, consisted of reciting the name of the Buddha over and over while caught up in a frenzied trance. The practice is said to have begun with priests Kūya and Ippen and to have been the ancestor of today's *Bon-odori* or dance performed at the mid-summer Bon Festival. In Kyoto the dance became a mob ritual so threatening to the authorities that it was banned in 1505. An observer in 1486 in Sakai near present-day Osaka noted that "all night they bang drums and clang bells and voices chanting the name of the Buddha move heaven and earth—it has become the latest fad."

---

†*Ibid.*, 121ff. The question of Musō's willing dilution of Zen practice and his competence in general is discussed in Akamatsu and Yampolsky, "Muromachi Zen and the Gozan System" in John W. Hall and Toyoda Takeshi, eds., *Japan in the Muromachi Age* (Berkeley: Univ. of California Press, 1977), 322–24.

### Ryūsen Reisai (?–1360)

Ryūsen was the illegitimate son of Emperor Go-Daigo (r. 1318–1339), whose ill-fated attempt to establish an independent court in 1331 led to the schism of the Northern and Southern Courts (1333–1392) that spans the Kamakura and Muromachi periods.

Ryūsen knew of his lineage, and his emotional involvement with the declining fortunes of the Southern Court must have been a personal one. His poem "Hearing About Another Revolt in Kansai," written while he was in Kamkura, reveals something of the intensity of his feelings on receiving news of one of the many battles that were being carried on by partisans of the two lines. The poet himself seems aware of the fact that his poems show unsual emotion for someone supposed to be a Zen monk.

### Ryūshū Shūtaku (1308–1388)

According to a legend, Ryūshū at birth had long hair and looked so frightening that his mother thought he was a devil and threw him out; his live was saved, however, when he was protected by a pair of white dogs. By the age of six he had been sent off to Musō Soseki to be brought up as a monk, a common practice with unwanted children. Another of Musō's disciples, Shun'oku Myōha, later to become the most politically powerful figure of Musō's line, was sent to Musō in the same year, 1313, at the age of three.

Ryūshū became noted for his extreme superstition, but has remained more famous for his skill at calligraphy and painting. Known also as a scholar, he boasted of his zealous studies as a youth, an excess that seems to have had a bad effect on his health—a perusal of his collected works leaves one with the impression that he wrote more poems on the subjects of illness and medicine than any other Gozan poet.

Ryūshū often warned his students away from literary pursuits, however, and it is said that when he discovered his disciples trying to make a collection of his sayings he flew into a rage and burned all the papers. He also refused all attempts by the court to bestow a "National Master" (*Kokushi*) title upon him, although he himself recorded a dream in which the mantle of the Chinese founder of his faction, Wu-chun Shih-fan, was passed on to him. He headed several important temples in his lifetime, but found himself in the middle of a nasty factional battle in Musō's line in 1377 on the side opposite Shun'oku Myōha. The uncomfortable affinity of the two monks ended with their deaths in the same year.

### Seiin Shunshō (1358–1422)

Very little is known of Seiin's life beyond the fact that he was a disciple of Zekkai Chūshin and became the twenty-third abbot of

Shōkokuji in Kyoto in 1414. He left a great deal of poetry, however, mostly poems intended to be written on paintings that they describe.

### Sesson Yūbai (1290–1346)

Sesson Yūbai left Japan at the age of eighteen to study in China, finally returning to Japan twenty-one years later. Before leaving Japan, he had studied with the Chinese priest I-shan, and his Chinese was said to be so perfect that, in the words of his disciple-biographer, "no one in China knew that he was a foreigner."

It is clear that someone in China knew. The Mongols, still smarting after two unsuccessful attempts to conquer Japan and therefore often capricious in their treatment of Japanese monks in China, threw Sesson in jail in 1314, perhaps on the same xenophobic suspicions of foreign spies that made the Japanese rulers temporarily exile Lan-hsi Tao-Lung half a century earlier. Sesson managed to escape beheading only by reciting four Zen poems, each beginning with a line of a poem composed by Wu-hsüeh Tsu-yüan under exactly similar circumstances some forty years earlier.

Released the same year he was jailed, Sesson lived for three years in Ch'ang-an until he was sent into exile in 1317 in the area that is now Szechuan Province. There he remained for ten years until the mass pardon customarily granted at the accession to the throne of a new Emperor—in this case, Jen-tsung, who was to rule less than a year. Although given the unprecedented honor of the abbacy of a large and important temple in Ch'ang-an, Sesson appears to have reconsidered the wisdom of further prolonging his stay in China and returned to Japan the following year, 1329. By the time of his death in Japan in 1346 he had headed several of the most important of the Gozan temples.

The only surviving poetry of Sesson's is contained in a collection of poems written during his exile to Szechuan, the *Bingashū*, "Collection from O-mei and Min". As might be expected under the circumstances, many of his poem are in the style of the T'ang Dynasty poet Tu Fu, who lived for many years in self-imposed exile in the same region.

### Tesshū Tokusai (?–1366)

Little is known of Tesshū's life. He went to China sometime between 1333 and 1351 after studying at Tenryūji in Kyoto, returning to Japan to study with Musō Soseki in the year of Musō's death. He was abbot of Manjuji in Kyoto, a Gozan Temple, for less than a year. Tesshū is best known today for his ink painting, especially of orchids.

### Tetsuan Dōshō (1260–1331)

Like many monks, Tetsuan never went to China—"A good thing for the Chinese he did not," said a contemporary, whose comment reflects the esteem in which Tetsuan's poetry was held in his own day. The statement is also one expression of the contradictory impulses felt by Japanese Zen monks toward China beginning about the second half of the fourteenth century, awed respect for the great tradition and its homeland alternating with a wistful nostalgia for an even more glorious past and increasingly tinged with contempt for the inglorious reality of China under Mongol domination.

The imagery in the second of Tetsuan's "Living in the Mountains" (p. 66) illustrates a critical aesthetic concept which, for lack of a better term, I have translated as "pleasingly stark." The words literally mean "plain and thin" and include everything that is the opposite of colorful, showy or gaudy. Yet the concept is positive in its associations, not negative; an aesthetic which, as the poet says, is perceived by the uninitiated as mere poverty (the usual meaning of the phrase "cold and sour"), it is an important concept derived from Sung dynasty critical literature dealing with art and poetry. The concept was first interpreted by the Gozan monks, and became highly influential in Japan in the development of Muromach period aesthetics, especially the taste for a quiet, subdued simplicity that dominated Zen poetry, ink painting, tea ceremony, and came to pervade the arts and crafts in general.

### Wu-hsüeh Tsu-yüan (Mugaku Sogen, 1226–1286)

After the death of Lan-hsi Tao-lung in 1278, the Regent Hōjō Tokimune (r. 1268–84) sent two Japanese monks to China with the task of inviting another Chinese master to Japan. Their first choice refused to make the journey pleading advanced age, but recommended Wu-hsüeh to take his place.

Wu-hsüeh arrived in Japan in 1279 between the two attempted Mongol invasions of Japan (1274 and 1281) and a mere six months after the fall of the Southern Sung dynasty to the Mongols. Wu-hsüeh himself had only barely escaped decapitation at the hands of Mongol soldiers while he was in China—so the legend goes—by reciting a particularly impressive Zen poem just as they were about to strike off his head.

In 1282, Tokimune made Wu-hsüeh head of the important Engakuji temple in Kamakura out of gratitude for the efficacy of the Chinese monk's prayers for the destruction of the Mongol invasion force that came to grief the year before.

Wu-hsüeh's poems translated here reveal the balance between poetic and didactic elements that characterizes early Gozan poetry. The ninth of his "Twenty-eight Songs of the Way, at White Cloud Hermitage" is typical of Zen poetry written on the eighth day of the twelfth month, the day on which the Buddha's enlightenment is celebrated and the end of the intensive winter zazen period called *Rōhatsu*. In such poetry, the poet often describes his quest for enlightenment in terms of an arduous passage over high mountain peaks and through winter snows, and the final failure of the will to repeat the achievements of the Buddha Shakyamuni and the first Zen Patriarch Bodhidharma. The "old monkey" in the last line of the poem is Bodhidharma himself, alone on the highest of all peaks in the worst weather.

For all the sternness associated with the Zen of the great Kamakura temples (and sometimes contrasted with the less rigorous, more Japanese Zen of the Kyoto temples), Wu-hsüeh was considered so motherly in the careful instruction he gave his disciples that his style of Zen was known as *roba* or "old woman" Zen.

### Zekkai Chūshin (1336–1405)

Zekkai seems in every way the complement of his friend Gidō Shūshin, perhaps even more nearly his opposite. Gidō was sociable to a fault, politically sensitive, tactful, and literary in the extreme. Zekkai, on the other hand, often led a nearly hermitic existence necessitated in part by his lack of social tact and political sensitivity; he also left behind a mere ten percent the number of poems Gidō did. Gidō never went to China, but Zekkai stayed there for ten years (1368–78) at the start of the Ming Dynasty that succeeded the Mongol rule.

By Chinese standards, Zekkai was much the better poet, astounding the Chinese themselves with a facility for antithesis and allusion that led a Chinese monk to observe (in a 1403 preface to Zekkai's works) that Zekkai's Chinese did not in the least smack of Japanese, as most of his countrymen's did. Perhaps it was these qualities that so attracted the Meiji writer Natsume Soseki, who, as he observed in a Chinese poem of 1915, always kept a volume of Zekkai's poetry on his desk.

In China, Zekkai studied with the most famous Ch'an masters, visited a Chinese friend who had recently returned from a two-year stay in Japan as Ming envoy (he was kept under house arrest in Kyoto the whole time, to the delight of the local monks who had a captive audience), and presented his teacher Musō's collection to the famous Ming writer Sung Lien (1310–1381) to ask for a preface. A fad among the Gozan monks for Chinese prefaces kept the Chinese literati busy and no doubt returned them a certain remuneration. Zekkai was even invited to the Imperial Palace in 1376 and received by the Emperor T'ai-tsu himself, who graciously wrote a poem in reply to one presented by Zekkai (at the Imperial command), an honor never granted any other Japanese.

After receiving such acclaim in China, Zekkai's homecoming in 1378

was something of a disappointment. He returned from a land just set-
tling down after the transition from Mongol to Chinese rule to a Japan
still embroiled in the civil wars between adherents of the Northern and
Southern courts. He arrived in Kyushu in the midst of fighting between
Imagawa Ryōshun, an important warrior man of letters and patron of
Zen, and the Kikuchi clan over lands in Satsuma province contested by
supporters of the Ashikagas on the one hand and adherents of the Southern Court at Yoshino on the other. If Zekkai's poems written while in
China often bewail the glories of a vanished past, couched in terms of
the epic battles of the Three Kingdoms, those following his arrival to
Japan lament the civil wars in terms of the equally epic battles between
the Taira and the Minamoto clans, and the final defeat of the Taira at
the battle of Dannoura in 1185.

Zekkai made his way from Kyushu to Kyoto, arriving in 1378 to find
his faction (Musō's line) divided and wrangling bitterly over the disposi-
tion of Rinsenji. He left Kyoto almost immediately for the quiet of a
small temple in the mountains of nearby Ōmi province to wait out the
troubles. To a friend Zekkai wrote, "Not one single day of rest have I
been able to enjoy since I returned from China."

By 1382, Gidō had managed to have Zekkai introduced to the Shogun
Yoshimitsu, but some personality conflict between the two seems to have
erupted almost immediately after. In his second poem on "Dwelling in the
Mountains," Zekkai alludes to the Shogun as a "haughty prince," and in the
years that followed Zekkai was to spend a good deal of his time in the
provinces around Kyoto in an attempt to keep out of the Shogun's way. By
1386, however, the two had mended their relationship enough that Zekkai
agreed to return to Kyoto to head the Ashikaga's family temple, Tōji-in.
After Gidō's death two years later Yoshimitsu came gradually to rely
increasingly on Zekkai for advice, and by the time of the suppression of the
Meitoku Rebellion in 1391, Yoshimitsu is reported to have gone forth to
battle wearing Zekkai's own Zen robes.

Zekkai subsequently held one high office after another until his
death in 1405. While it was Gidō that held Musō's faction together long
enough to guarantee its continued dominance of the Gozan, most of the
famous poets that follow in this volume were in Zekkai's line rather than
Gidō's.

# INDEX OF POEMS
## ARRANGED CONSECUTIVELY BY POET